FIRST
FRENCH
PICTURE DICTIONARY

 2nd CANADIAN EDITION

DK

Second Canadian edition

DK Canada
Editor, Canada Barbara Campbell
Canadian French Consultant Agnès Roux

DK India
Editor Deeksha Saikia
Art Editor Shreya Sadhan
Senior DTP Designer Shanker Prasad
Picture Researcher Aditya Katyal
Jacket Designer Suhita Dharamjit
Managing Jackets Editor Saloni Talwar
Pre-production Manager Balwant Singh
Managing Editor Kingshuk Ghoshal
Senior Managing Art Editor
Romi Chakraborty

DK UK
Producer, pre-production Luca Frassinetti
Producer Rita Sinha
Managing Editor Linda Esposito
Managing Art Editor Michael Duffy
Publisher Andrew Macintyre
Publishing Director Jonathan Metcalf
Associate Publishing Director Liz Wheeler
Design Director Stuart Jackman

Original Canadian edition
Project Editor Anna Harrison
Editors Elise See Tai, Lucy Heaver
Editor, Canada Julia Roles
Project Art Editors Ann Cannings, Emy Manby
DTP Designer David McDonald
Production Harriet Maxwell
Translator Chantal Lamarque with
Elise Bradbury
Managing Editor Scarlett O'Hara

Second Canadian Edition, 2015

Copyright © 2005, 2009, 2015
Dorling Kindersley Limited

A Penguin Random House Company
15 16 17 10 9 8 7 6 5 4 3 2 1
001–276737–Aug/2015

DK Canada
320 Front Street West, 11th Floor
Toronto, Ontario M5V 3B6

Library and Archives Canada Cataloguing
in Publication
    DK first French picture dictionary. --
2nd Canadian edition.
ISBN 978-1-55363-251-1 (pbk.)
    1. Picture dictionaries, French--Juvenile
literature. 2. Picture dictionaries, English--Juvenile
literature. 3. French language--Dictionaries,
Juvenile--English. 4. English language--
Dictionaries, Juvenile--French. I. Title: French
picture dictionary. II. Title: First French
picture dictionary.
PC2629.D54 2005   j443'.21   C2005-900709-5

Colour reproduction by Colourscan, Singapore
Printed and bound in China by Hung Hing
Printing Group Ltd.

A WORLD OF IDEAS:
SEE ALL THERE IS TO KNOW
www.dk.com

Contents

How to use this dictionary

Find out how you can get the most from your dictionary. At the beginning of the book there are Topic pages. These include lots of useful words on a particular subject, such as *Pets* and *In the Park*. Each word has its translation and help on how to pronounce it. The words on the Topic pages can be found in the English A–Z and in the French A–Z. There are lots of other useful words here too. The verbs are in another section. At the back of the book there is a list of useful phrases for you to use when you practise your French with your friends.

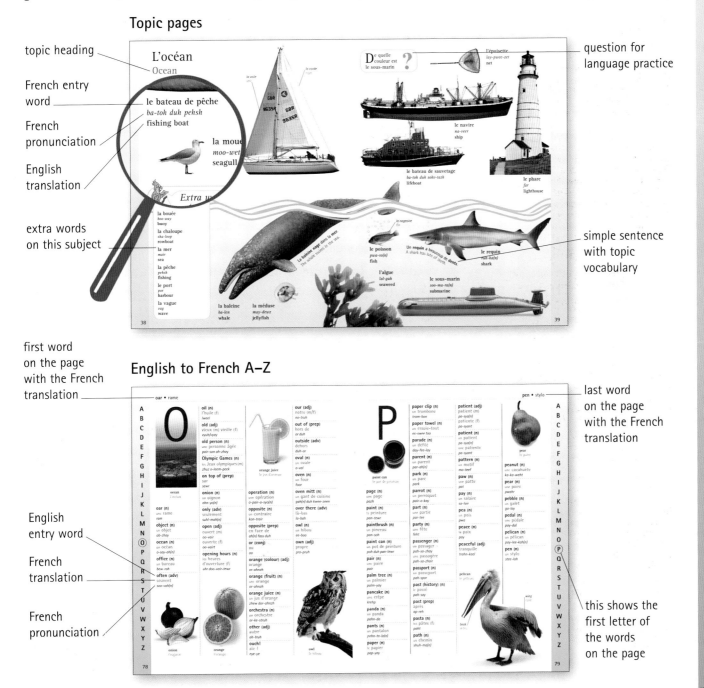

Topic pages

topic heading

French entry word

French pronunciation

English translation

extra words on this subject

question for language practice

simple sentence with topic vocabulary

first word on the page with the French translation

English to French A–Z

English entry word

French translation

French pronunciation

last word on the page with the French translation

this shows the first letter of the words on the page

Tout sur moi
All about me

*Je suis **grande**.*
I'm tall.

le père
pair
father

la mère
mair
mother

*Voici ma **famille**.*
This is my family.

le bébé
bay-bay
baby

la sœur
suhr
sister

le frère
frair
brother

le grand-père
grandfather

la grand-mère
grandmother

les grands-parents
grah(n)-par-ah(n)
grandparents

l'enfant
lahn-fah(n)
child

la tante
tahnt
aunt

l'oncle
lonk-luh
uncle

*Nous sommes **contentes**!*
We're happy!

contente
kon-tahnt
happy

*Thomas est **en colère**.*
Thomas is angry.

en colère
ah(n) ko-lehr
angry

4

les cheveux
shuh-vuh
hair

le cou
koo
neck

le coude
kood
elbow

la dent
dah(n)
tooth

le dos
do
back

la famille
fa-mee-ye
family

le genou
zhuh-noo
knee

le sourcil
soor-seel
eyebrow

le visage
vee-zazh
face

la tête
teht
head

l'oreille
lo-raye
ear

l'épaule
lay-pohl
shoulder

le bras
bra
arm

l'estomac
les-to-ma
stomach

la main
ma(n)
hand

le doigt
dwa
finger

l'œil
luh-ye
eye

le nez
nay
nose

la bouche
boosh
mouth

Je **m'étire.**
I'm stretching.

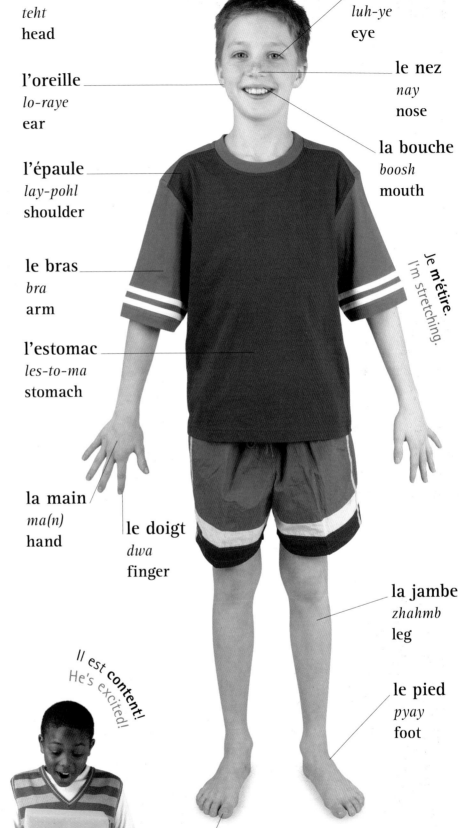

la jambe
zhahmb
leg

le pied
pyay
foot

l'orteil
lor-teye
toe

Je **pleure** quand je suis **triste.**
I cry when I'm sad.

triste
treest
sad

Il est **content!**
He's excited!

excité
ek-see-tay
excited

De quelle
couleur
sont tes yeux

Les vêtements
Clothes

le bouton
button

les bas
bah
socks

la chemise
shuh-meez
shirt

le jean
jeen
jeans

Extra words to learn

le chandail
shahn-da-ye
sweater

la chaussure
shoh-soor
shoe

le gant
gah(n)
glove

les lunettes
lew-net
glasses

la pantoufle
pahn-too-fluh
slipper

le pyjama
pee-zha-ma
pajamas

la robe
rob
dress

les sous-vêtements
soo-veht-mah(n)
underwear

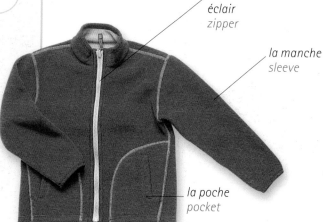

la fermeture éclair
zipper

la manche
sleeve

la poche
pocket

le polar
po-lar
fleece

Mon **manteau** me tient **chaud**.
My coat keeps me warm.

le foulard
foo-lahr
scarf

les espadrilles
ehs-pa-dree-ye
running shoes

le gant
glove

le manteau
mahn-toh
coat

la ceinture
belt

le tee-shirt
tee-shirt
T-shirt

le short
short
shorts

le maillot de bain
ma-yoh duh ba(n)
bathing suit

le pantalon
pahn-ta-lo(n)
pants

le blouson
bloo-zo(n)
jacket

la capuche
hood

la jupe
zhewp
skirt

l'imperméable
lam-pair-may-a-bluh
raincoat

le jean
jeans

Les **jeans** et les **espadrilles** sont mes **vêtements** préférés.
My favourite clothes are jeans and running shoes.

les bottes
bot
boots

A imes-tu
porter
des espadrilles ?

7

La cuisine
Kitchen

la casserole
saucepan

la poêle
pwal
frying pan

l'assiette
la-syet
plate

le four
oven

la cuisinière
kwee-zeen-yair
stove

la cuillère
kwee-yehr
spoon

la tasse
tahss
mug

le livre
book

le torchon
tor-sho(n)
dish towel

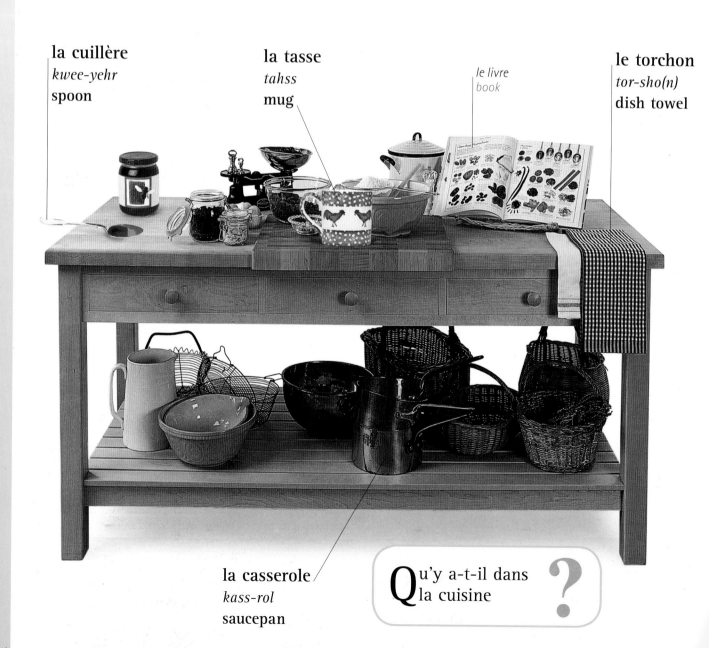

la casserole
kass-rol
saucepan

Qu'y a-t-il dans
la cuisine **?**

8

Merci de faire la vaisselle.
Thank you for washing the dishes.

le placard
cupboard

l'évier
layv-yay
sink

le congélateur
freezer

le réfrigérateur
ray-free-zhair-a-tuhr
fridge

Extra words to learn

la bouilloire
booy-wahr
kettle

la cruche
krewsh
jug

le fer à repasser
fair ah ruh-pah-say
iron

le grille-pain
gree-ye-pa(n)
toaster

la machine à laver
ma-sheen ah la-vay
washing machine

le plateau
pla-toh
tray

la poubelle
poo-bell
garbage can

la tasse
tahss
cup

le couteau
koo-toh
knife

la fourchette
foor-shet
fork

le tablier
tab-lee-yay
apron

le gant de cuisine
gah(n) duh kwee-zeen
oven mitt

le verre
vair
glass

Aimes-tu faire de la pâtisserie?
Do you like baking?

La salle de bains
Bathroom

le peigne
pain-ye
comb

la baignoire
bayn-wahr
bathtub

C'est amusant de faire des **bulles**.
It's fun making bubbles.

le jouet
zhoo-way
toy

l'eau
loh
water

Je mets du **dentifrice** sur ma **brosse à dents**.
I put toothpaste on my toothbrush.

l'éponge
lay-ponzh
sponge

les serviettes
sair-vee-et
towels

le dentifrice
dahn-tee-freess
toothpaste

le tube
tube

la brosse à dents
bros ah dah(n)
toothbrush

Combien d'objets jaunes y a-t-il sur cette page ?

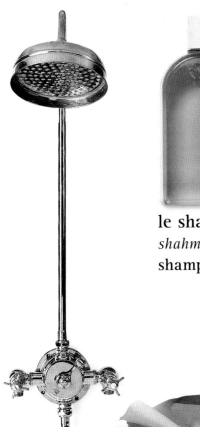

le shampooing
shahm-pwa(n)
shampoo

le miroir
meer-wahr
mirror

Extra words to learn

la brosse à cheveux
bros ah shuh-vuh
hairbrush

la buée
bway
steam

le maquillage
ma-kee-yazh
makeup

les papier-mouchoirs
pap-yay moosh-wahr
tissues

se laver
suh la-vay
washing

la débarbouillette
day-bar-boo-yet
facecloth

la douche
doosh
shower

le papier hygiénique
pap-yay ee-zhen-eek
toilet paper

le savon
sa-vo(n)
soap

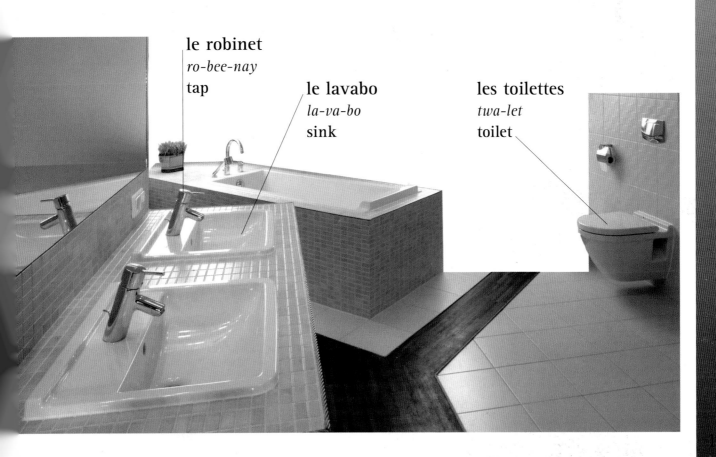

le robinet
ro-bee-nay
tap

le lavabo
la-va-bo
sink

les toilettes
twa-let
toilet

le réveil
ray-vaye
alarm clock

le lit
lee
bed

l'oreiller
lo-ray-yay
pillow

la couette
koo-et
duvet

la chaise
shehz
chair

Ma chambre
My bedroom

la commode
kom-mod
chest of drawers

Je **dors** dans mon **lit**.
I sleep in my bed.

le jeu électronique
zhuh ay-lek-tro-neek
computer game

Nous **jouons** à un **jeu de plateau**.
We're playing a board game.

Mon **chat dort** sous mon **lit**.
My cat sleeps under my bed.

la moquette
moh-ket
carpet

Qu'y a-t-il dans l'armoire?
What's in the wardrobe?

La **moquette** est bleue.
The carpet is blue.

les échecs
chess

le tapis
ta-pee
rug

les livres
leev-ruh
books

Je sais jouer de la **guitare**.
I can play the guitar.

l'armoire
larm-wahr
wardrobe

la guitare
ghee-tar
guitar

le cintre
san-truh
coat hanger

la lampe
lahmp
lamp

le miroir
meer-wahr
mirror

Le jardin
Garden

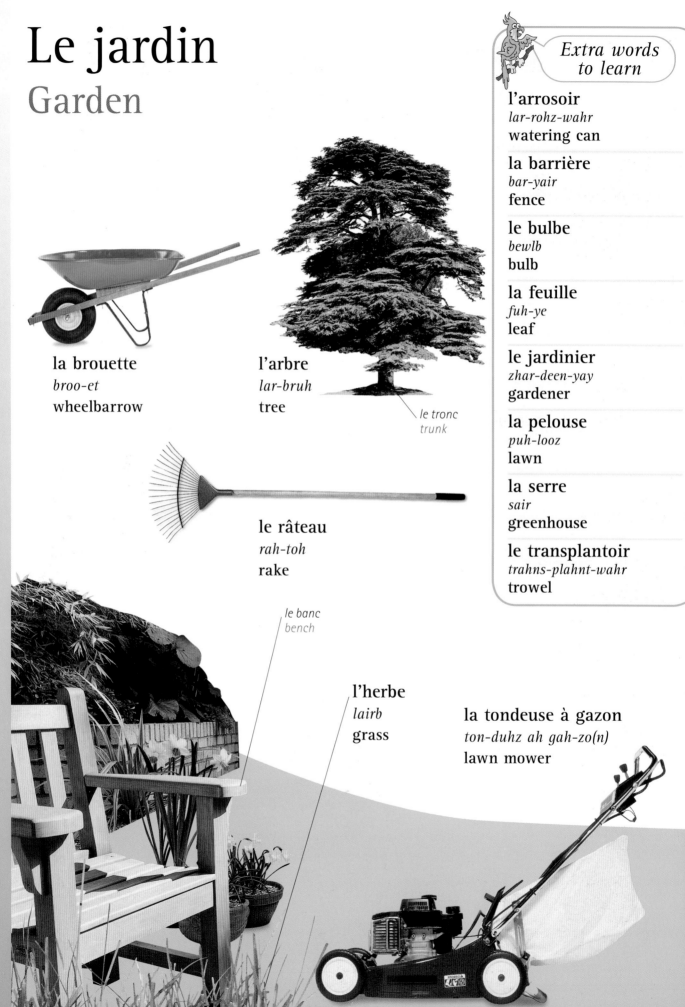

Extra words to learn

l'arrosoir
lar-rohz-wahr
watering can

la barrière
bar-yair
fence

le bulbe
bewlb
bulb

la feuille
fuh-ye
leaf

le jardinier
zhar-deen-yay
gardener

la pelouse
puh-looz
lawn

la serre
sair
greenhouse

le transplantoir
trahns-plahnt-wahr
trowel

la brouette
broo-et
wheelbarrow

l'arbre
lar-bruh
tree

le tronc
trunk

le râteau
rah-toh
rake

le banc
bench

l'herbe
lairb
grass

la tondeuse à gazon
ton-duhz ah gah-zo(n)
lawn mower

14

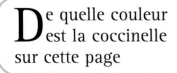

De quelle couleur
est la coccinelle
sur cette page **?**

l'aile
wing

le papillon
pa-pee-yo(n)
butterfly

l'escargot
les-kar-goh
snail

le ver
vair
worm

l'abeille
la-baye
bee

la graine
grehn
seed

la coccinelle
kok-see-nel
ladybug

Les **fleurs poussent** dans le **jardin**.
Flowers are growing in the garden.

Marie **creuse** dans le **jardin**.
Marie is digging in the garden.

la fleur
fluhr
flower

la chenille
shuh-nee-ye
caterpillar

la terre
tair
soil

la pelle
pel
spade

La vie en ville
City life

l'autobus
lohto-bews
bus

la maison
may-zo(n)
house

Quelle heure **Q**est-il sur l'horloge bleue

le gratte-ciel
grat-syel
skyscraper

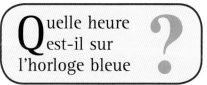

Les **villes** ont des **hauts bâtiments** appelés **gratte-ciels**.
Cities have tall buildings called skyscrapers.

l'horloge
lor-lozh
clock

les appartements
ap-par-tuh-mah(n)
apartments

la rue
rew
street

le magasin
ma-ga-za(n)
store

l'arrêt d'autobus
lar-reh dohto-bews
bus stop

l'autoroute
loh-toh-root
highway

la banque
bahnk
bank

le café
ka-fay
café

la gare
gar
station

la route
root
road

le trottoir
trot-wahr
sidewalk

l'usine
lew-zeen
factory

le téléphone
tay-lay-fon
phone

le panneau de signalisation
pan-noh duh seen-ya-lee-za-syo(n)
sign

les feux de signalisation
fuh duh seen-ya-lee-za-syo(n)
traffic lights

le cinéma
see-nay-ma
movie theatre

le réverbère
ray-vair-bair
street light

le carrefour
kar-foor
crossing

le taxi
tak-see
taxi

l'hôtel
lo-tel
hotel

Au parc
In the park

le cerf-volant
sair-vo-lah(n)
kite

**la corde
à sauter**
kord ah soh-tay
skipping rope

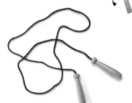

**la planche
à roulettes**
plahnsh a roo-leht
skateboard

les fleurs
fluhr
flowers

le tourniquet
toor-nee-kay
carousel

la fille
fee-ye
girl

J'adore **sauter à la corde**!
I love skipping.

As-tu un cerf-volant?
Have you got a kite?

l'arbre
lar-bruh
tree

Les **oiseaux** chantent.
The birds are singing.

la balançoire
ba-lahn-swahr
swing

le garçon
gar-so(n)
boy

Trois **enfants** jouent sur le **tourniquet**.
Three children are playing on the carousel.

Mon **jeu** préféré est le **soccer**.
My favourite game is soccer.

le ballon
ba-lo(n)
ball

le papillon
pa-pee-yo(n)
butterfly

l'oiseau
lwa-zoh
bird

le vélo
vay-lo
bike

la feuille
fuh-ye
leaf

l'herbe
lairb
grass

Les passe-temps
Hobbies

Mes **fleurs** poussent.
My flowers are growing.

Mathilde **s'entraîne** tous les jours.
Mathilde practises every day.

faire du camping
fair dew kahm-peeng
camping

Je suis **prête** à aller nager.
I'm ready to go swimming.

la natation
na-ta-syo(n)
swimming

le jardinage
zhar-dee-nazh
gardening

jouer d'un instrument
zhoo-ay dan an-strew-mah(n)
playing an instrument

observer les oiseaux
ob-zair-vay layz wa-zoh
birdwatching

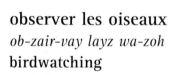

faire de la danse
fair duh la dahnss
dancing

20

le chant
shah(n)
singing

collectionner
kol-lek-syo-nay
collecting

le dessin
de-sa(n)
drawing

faire la cuisine
fair la kwee-zeen
cooking

faire du patin à roues alignées
fair dew pa-ta(n) ah roo ah-lin-yay
rollerblading

faire du théâtre
fair dew tay-a-truh
acting

faire du vélo
fair dew vay-lo
cycling

la lecture
lek-tewr
reading

l'écriture
lay-kree-tewr
writing

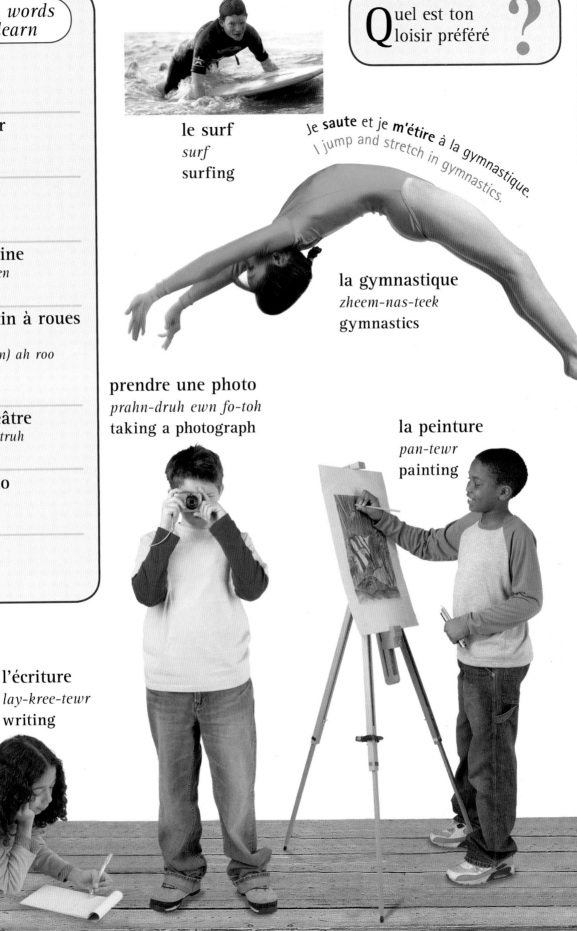

le surf
surf
surfing

Quel est ton
Qloisir préféré **?**

Je **saute** et je **m'étire** à la gymnastique.
I jump and stretch in gymnastics.

la gymnastique
zheem-nas-teek
gymnastics

prendre une photo
prahn-druh ewn fo-toh
taking a photograph

la peinture
pan-tewr
painting

La nourriture
Food

la peau
skin

l'orange
lor-ahnzh
orange

la pomme
pom
apple

la graine
seed

le melon d'eau
muh-lo(n) doh
watermelon

la banane
ba-nan
banana

la tomate
tom-at
tomato

la carotte
ka-rot
carrot

la laitue
lay-tew
lettuce

le chou
shoo
cabbage

Nous **mangeons** des **pâtes**!
We're eating pasta!

l'assiette
plate

le verre
glass

Un **ananas** est un **fruit.**
A pineapple is a fruit.

le couteau
knife

la fourchette
fork

la chaise
chair

la table
table

l'ananas
lan-an-ass
pineapple

la pomme de terre
pom duh tair
potato

l'œuf
luhf
egg

le yogourt
yoh-goor
yogourt

le lait
lay
milk

la confiture
kon-fee-tewr
jam

Que manges-tu au petit-déjeuner **?**

J'aime le **pain** avec du **miel**.
I like bread with honey.

le pain
pa(n)
bread

le beurre
buhr
butter

le miel
myel
honey

Extra words to learn

le biscuit
bee-skwee
cookie

la farine
far-een
flour

le fruit
frwee
fruit

le légume
lay-gewm
vegetable

l'oignon
lohn-yo(n)
onion

le poulet
poo-lay
chicken

la salade
sal-ad
salad

les spaghettis
spa-get-ee
spaghetti

le sucre
soo-kruh
sugar

les pâtes
paht
pasta

le riz
rice

la viande
vyanhnd
meat

Les courses
Shopping

Aimes-tu
Afaire
les courses **?**

le marché
mar-shay
market

le prix
price

l'argent
lar-zhahn
money

le sac
sak
shopping bag

Je dois acheter des œufs.
I've got to buy some eggs.

Nous attendons dans la queue.
We're waiting in line.

le panier
pan-yay
basket

le chariot
shar-yoh
shopping cart

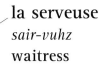

la serveuse
sair-vuhz
waitress

le café
ka-fay
café

la liste de courses
leest duh koorss
shopping list

le supermarché
soo-pair-mar-shay
supermarket

Elle a beaucoup de **sacs**!
She's got lots of bags!

l'acheteuse
lash-tuhz
shopper

la boulangerie
boo-lahn-zhree
bakery

la librairie
leeb-rair-ee
bookshop

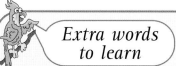

Extra words to learn

la caisse
kehss
checkout

en espèces
ah(n) es-pehss
(in) cash

la facture
fak-tuh-ruh
bill

faire les courses
fair lay koorss
to go shopping

le magasin
ma-ga-za(n)
store

le prix
pree
price

le reçu
ruh-sew
receipt

le vendeur
vahn-duhr
sales person

la boisson
bwa-so(n)
drink

les sandwichs
sahnd-weetsh
sandwiches

les cartes d'anniversaire
kart dan-ee-vair-sair
birthday cards

les bougies
boo-zhee
candles

le gâteau d'anniversaire
gah-toh dan-ee-vair-sair
birthday cake

À la fête
At the party

Nous aimons danser.
We like dancing.

le lecteur de CD
lek-tuhr duh say-day
CD player

le magicien
ma-zhee-sya(n)
magician

Vois-tu le gâteau d'anniversaire?
Can you see the birthday cake?

les décorations
day-ko-ra-syo(n)
decorations

Bon anniversaire!
Happy birthday!

Je veux **ouvrir** les **cadeaux**.
I want to open the gifts.

les cadeaux
ka-doh
gifts

Vois-tu les **cartes d'anniversaire**?
Can you see the birthday cards?

les ballons
bal-o(n)
balloons

l'appareil photo
lap-pa-ray fo-toh
camera

les biscuits
bee-skwee
cookies

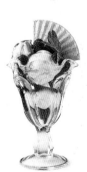

la crème glacée
krehm glasay
ice cream

les bonbons
bo(n)-bo(n)
candies

27

Temps libre
Free time

le jeu de plateau
zhuh duh pla-toh
board game

le ballon
bal-o(n)
ball

le robot
ro-boh
robot

les dés
day
dice

l'ordinateur portable
lor-dee-na-tuhr
por-ta-bluh
laptop

Extra words to learn

cache-cache
kash-kash
hide-and-seek

les cubes
kewb
toy blocks

le jeu
zhuh
game

le jouet
zhoo-way
toy

la marionnette
mar-yon-net
puppet

le masque
mask
mask

partir en vacances
par-teer ah(n) vak-ahns
going on vacation

la poupée
poo-pay
doll

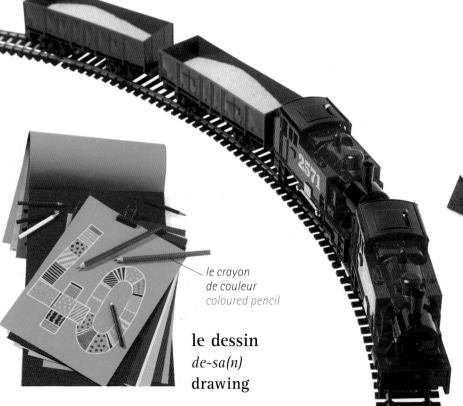

le crayon de couleur
coloured pencil

le dessin
de-sa(n)
drawing

le casse-tête
kahs-teht
puzzle

le train
tra(n)
train

les cartes
kart
cards

les CD
say-day
CDs

le lecteur MP3
lek-tuhr em-pay-trwa
MP3 player

le jeu électronique
zhuh ay-lek-tro-neek
computer game

le casque
helmet

Il **bouge** très vite!
He moves really fast!

Nous adorons la **glissade** d'eau.
We love the waterslide.

faire du patin à roues alignées
fair dew pa-ta(n) ah roo ah-lin-yay
rollerblading

Aimes-tu
les jeux
électroniques **?**

la glissade d'eau
glee-sad doh
waterslide

aller au cinéma
ah-lay oh see-nay-ma
going to the movies

le parc d'attractions
park dah-track-syo(n)
fairground

Les moyens de transport
Transport

l'avion
lav-yo(n)
airplane

le traversier
tra-vehr-syay
ferry

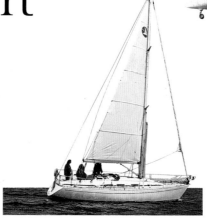

le bateau à voiles
ba-toh ah vwal
sailboat

le taxi
tak-see
taxi

le camion
kam-yo(n)
truck

le vélo
vay-lo
bike

Les **gens** voyagent en **autobus**.
People travel by bus.

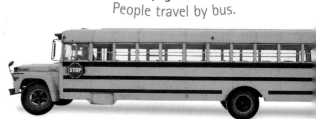

l'autobus
lohto-bews
bus

Pour les secours
To the rescue

l'échelle
ladder

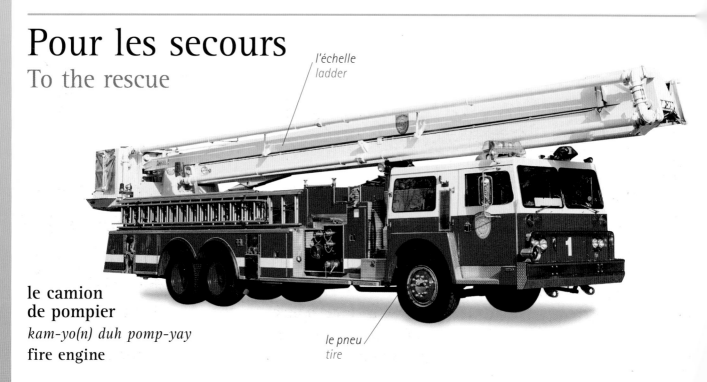

**le camion
de pompier**
kam-yo(n) duh pomp-yay
fire engine

le pneu
tire

le panier
basket

*Une **montgolfière** vole dans le ciel.*
A hot-air balloon is flying in the sky.

la montgolfière
mohn-golf-yair
hot-air balloon

le train
tra(n)
train

les bagages
luggage

la voiture
vwah-tewr
car

la moto
moh-toh
motorcycle

la roue
wheel

Extra words to learn

l'autocar
lohto-kar
coach

le billet
bee-yay
ticket

la camionnette
kam-yon-net
van

le carburant
kar-bew-rah(n)
fuel

la fusée
few-zay
space rocket

le garage
gar-azh
garage

l'horaire
lor-air
timetable

le voyage
vwa-yazh
journey

l'hélicoptère de police
lay-lee-kop-tair duh po-leess
police helicopter

Combien de roues y a-t-il sur cette page ?

la voiture de police
vwa-tewr duh po-leess
police car

l'ambulance
lahm-bew-lahnss
ambulance

Les animaux de la jungle
Jungle animals

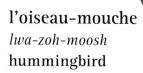

l'oiseau-mouche
lwa-zoh-moosh
hummingbird

l'aile
wing

le papillon
pa-pee-yo(n)
butterfly

le chimpanzé
shahm-pahn-zay
chimpanzee

la chauve-souris
shohv soo-ree
bat

la fourmi
foor-mee
ant

l'araignée
lar-ehn-yay
spider

le gorille
go-ree-ye
gorilla

le papillon de nuit
pa-pee-yo(n) duh nwee
moth

le crocodile
kro-ko-deel
crocodile

Quels animaux peuvent voler sur cette page **?**

Le toucan prend la **nourriture** avec son **bec**.
The toucan gets food with its beak.

l'œil
eye

le bec
beak

le toucan
too-kah(n)
toucan

la griffe
claw

le perroquet
pair-o-kay
parrot

Extra words to learn

l'aigle
lay-gluh
eagle

l'arbre
lar-bruh
tree

la forêt tropicale
for-eh tro-pee-kal
rainforest

l'insecte
lan-sekt
insect

le lézard
lay-zar
lizard

le mammifère
ma-mee-fair
mammal

l'oiseau
lwa-zoh
bird

le scarabée
ska-ra-bay
beetle

le serpent
sair-pah(n)
snake

la grenouille
gruh-noo-ye
frog

la patte
foot

les rayures
stripes

les taches
spots

le tigre
tee-gruh
tiger

le léopard
lay-o-par
leopard

Les animaux du monde
World animals

le koala
ko-a-la
koala

le chevreuil
shuh-vruh-ye
deer

la patte
paw

le lion
lee-yo(n)
lion

le panda
pahn-da
panda

La **girafe** a un long **cou**!
The giraffe has a long neck!

la girafe
zhee-raf
giraffe

l'ours polaire
loorss po-lair
polar bear

le bec
beak

la queue
tail

le pingouin
pah(n)-gwa(h)
penguin

l'alligator
lal-ee-gah-tor
alligator

le babouin
ba-bwa(n)
baboon

la chauve-souris
shohv soo-ree
bat

le faucon
foh-ko(n)
hawk

le loup
loo
wolf

le pélican
pay-lee-kah(n)
pelican

le renard
ruh-nar
fox

la tortue de mer
tor-tew duh mair
turtle

Combien d'oiseaux ya-t-il sur cette page ?

le chameau
sha-moh
camel

L'**éléphant prend** la **nourriture** avec sa **trompe**.
The elephant gets food with its trunk.

les rayures
stripes

le zèbre
zeh-bruh
zebra

la trompe
trunk

l'éléphant
lay-lay-fah(n)
elephant

le kangourou
kahn-goo-roo
kangaroo

la queue
tail

la griffe
claw

l'ours
loorss
bear

le dauphin
doh-fa(n)
dolphin

la palme
flipper

le rhinocéros
ree-no-say-ros
rhinoceros

35

À la ferme
On the farm

le tracteur
trak-tuhr
tractor

le chien de berger
shya(n) duh bair-zhay
sheepdog

le champ
shah(m)
field

le blé
blay
wheat

les agneaux
an-yoh
lambs

La **fermière** utilise le **tracteur**.
The farmer uses a tractor.

la fermière
fairm-yair
farmer

le mouton
moo-to(n)
sheep

la moissonneuse-batteuse
mwa-son-nuhz bat-tuhz
combine harvester

la barrière
bar-yair
fence

le canard
ka-nar
duck

Les **bébés des vaches** sont appelés des **veaux**.
Young cows are called calves.

Le **poussin** est **près de** sa **mère**.
The chick is near to its mother.

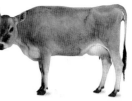

la vache
vash
cow

le foin
fwa(n)
hay

le cheval
shuh-val
horse

le poulet
poo-lay
chicken

les canetons
ka-nuh-to(n)
ducklings

37

L'océan
Ocean

le bateau de pêche
ba-toh duh pehsh
fishing boat

la mouette
moo-wet
seagull

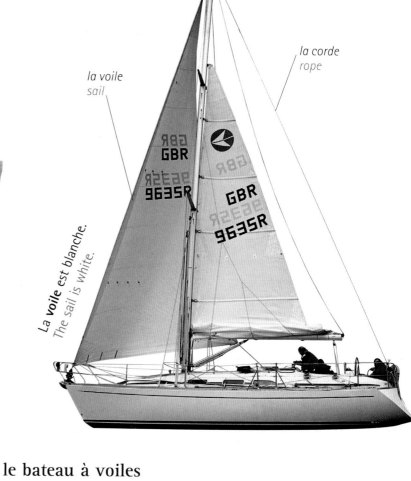

la voile
sail

la corde
rope

La **voile** est blanche.
The sail is white.

le bateau à voiles
ba-toh ah vwal
sailboat

Extra words to learn

l'ancre
lahn-kruh
anchor

la bouée
boo-way
buoy

la chaloupe
sha-loop
rowboat

la mer
mair
sea

la pêche
pehsh
fishing

le port
por
harbour

la vague
vag
wave

La **baleine nage** dans la **mer.**
The whale swims in the sea.

la baleine
ba-len
whale

la méduse
may-dewz
jellyfish

De quelle couleur est le sous-marin ?

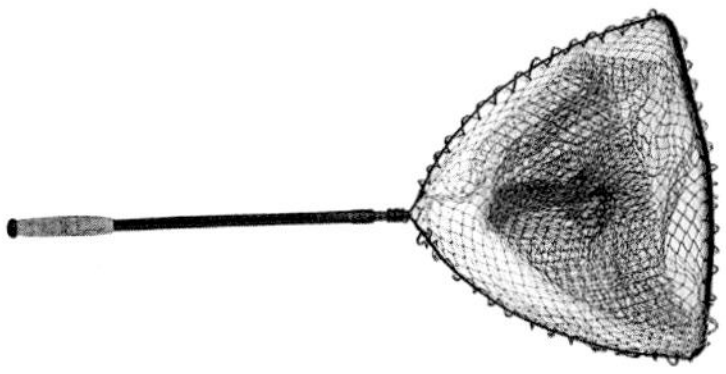

l'épuisette
lay-pwee-zet
net

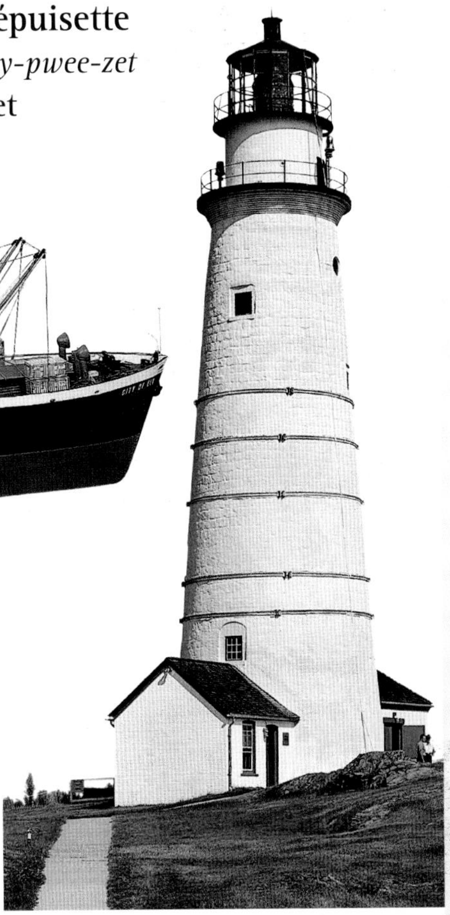

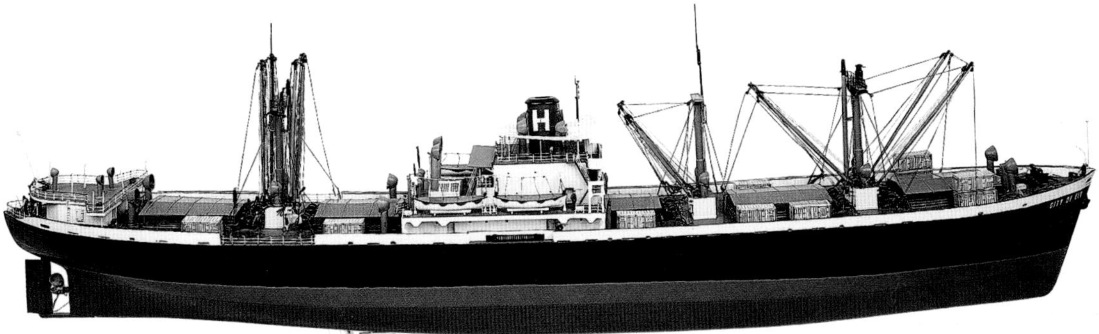

le navire
na-veer
ship

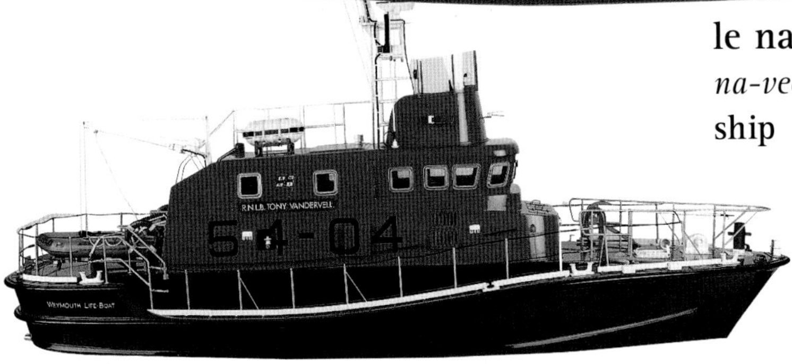
54-04

le bateau de sauvetage
ba-toh duh sohv-tazh
lifeboat

le phare
far
lighthouse

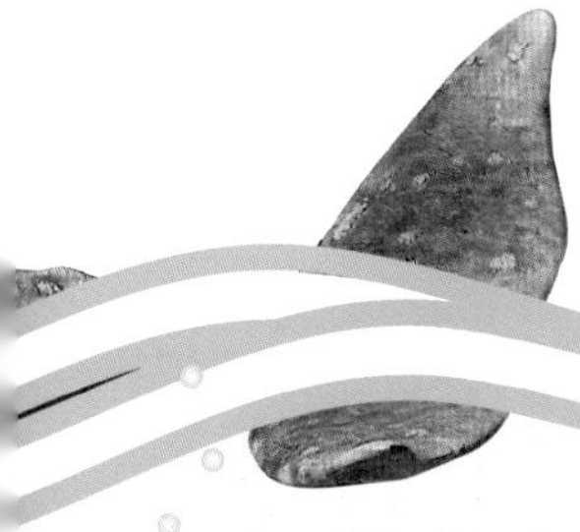

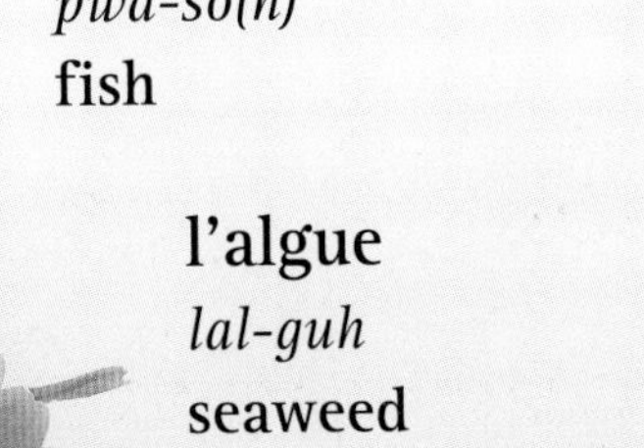
la nageoire
fin

le poisson
pwa-so(n)
fish

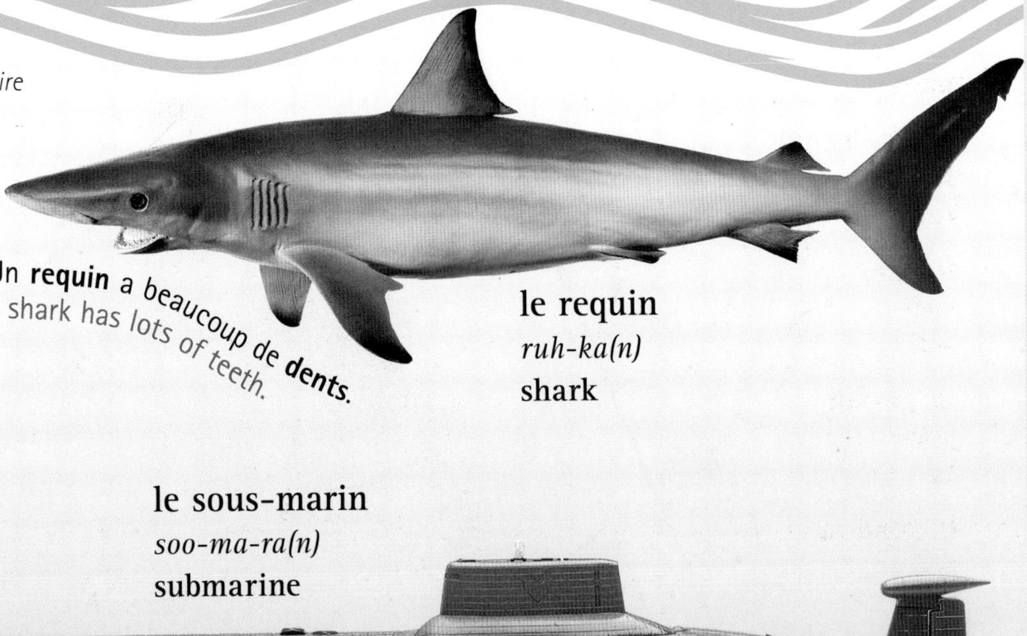

Un **requin** a beaucoup de **dents**.
A shark has lots of teeth.

le requin
ruh-ka(n)
shark

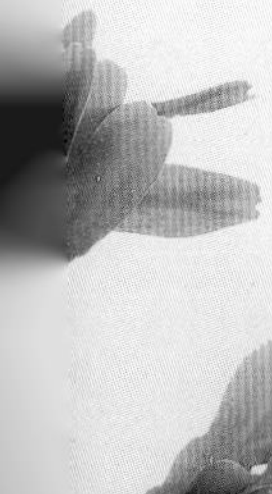

l'algue
lal-guh
seaweed

le sous-marin
soo-ma-ra(n)
submarine

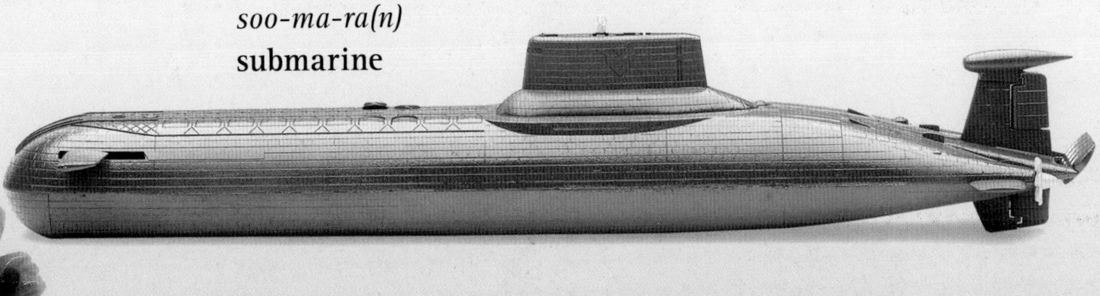

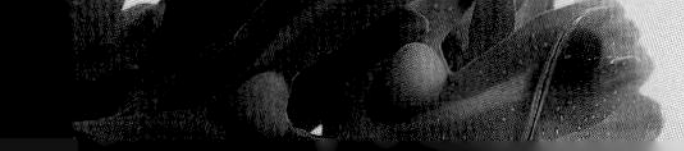

La nature
Nature

Le nénuphar pousse dans l'eau.
The water lily grows in the water.

la libellule
lee-bel-lewl
dragonfly

le nénuphar
nay-new-far
water lily

le canard
ka-nar
duck

le bec
beak

la plante
plahnt
plant

Beaucoup d'animaux vivent près des étangs.
Many animals live near ponds.

le cygne
seen-ye
swan

le crapaud
kra-poh
toad

Les **têtards nagent** dans les **étangs**.
Tadpoles swim in ponds.

Combien de nénuphars y a-t-il dans l'étang ?

le nid
nee
nest

les têtards
the-tar
tadpoles

l'antenne
antenna

la guêpe
gehp
wasp

l'aile
wing

la mouche
moosh
fly

l'étang
lay-tah(n)
pond

le hibou
ee-boo
owl

la grenouille
gruh-noo-ye
frog

Extra words to learn

l'eau
loh
water

l'habitat
la-bee-ta
habitat

le héron
air-o(n)
heron

l'insecte
lan-sekt
insect

le lapin
lap-a(n)
rabbit

la mauvaise herbe
moh-vayz airb
weed

l'oiseau
lwa-zoh
bird

le papillon
pa-pee-yo(n)
butterfly

41

le seau
soh
bucket

la pelle
pel
spade

le crabe
krab
crab

le coquillage
ko-kee-yazh
shell

les galets
ga-lay
pebbles

À la plage
At the beach

J'adore **nager** dans la **mer!**
I love swimming in the sea!

Aimes-tu **aller** à la **plage?**
Do you like going to the beach?

Je joue sous mon **parasol.**
I'm playing under my umbrella.

le parasol
umbrella

la roche
rosh
rock

la crème solaire
suntan lotion

les mouettes
moo-wet
seagulls

Nous adorons jouer avec le **sable**.
We love playing in the sand.

le maillot de bain
bathing suit

l'etoile de mer
lay-twal duh mair
starfish

la crème glacée
krehm glasay
ice cream

l'algue
lal-guh
seaweed

J'aime m'étendre au **soleil**.
I like to lie in the sun.

les lunettes
de natation
llew-net duh
na-ta-syo(n)
swim goggles

le chapeau
de soleil
sha-poh duh
so-laye
sunhat

la chaise
longue
shayz long-uh
deck chair

le sable
sah-bluh
sand

le château
de sable
sha-toh duh
sah-bluh
sandcastle

L'école
School

les ciseaux
see-zoh
scissors

les crayons de couleur
kra-yo(n) duh koo-luhr
coloured pencils

le tableau noir
tab-loh nwahr
blackboard

la règle
reh-gluh
ruler

la gomme à effacer
gom ah eh-fas-say
eraser

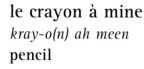

le crayon à mine
kray-o(n) ah meen
pencil

le stylo
stee-loh
pen

le carnet
notebook

le bureau
bew-roh
desk

Je fais mes devoirs à mon **bureau**.
I do my homework at my desk.

Vois-tu la pomme dans la **boîte à lunch**?
Can you see the apple in the lunch box?

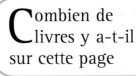

Combien de livres y a-t-il sur cette page **?**

la boîte à lunch
bwat ah lunch
lunch box

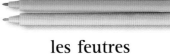

les feutres
fuh-truh
felt-tip pens

Trouve ton **pays** sur le **globe**.
Find your country on the globe.

le cahier
ka-yay
exercise book

le sac d'école —
school bag

le globe
glob
globe

les livres
leev-ruh
books

l'uniforme scolaire
lew-nee-form sko-lair
school uniform

l'ordinateur
lor-dee-na-tuhr
computer

Les sports
Sports

Je porte un **casque**.
I'm wearing a helmet.

le casque
helmet

la roue
wheel

le ski
skee
skiing

la raquette
rak-et
racket

faire du vélo
fair dew vay-lo
cycling

**le patinage
sur glace**
*pa-tee-nazh
sewr glass*
ice skating

la gymnastique
zheem-nas-teek
gymnastics

Nous **jouons** au **basketball**.
We're playing basketball.

le tee-shirt
T-shirt

le short
shorts

Delphine **veut marquer** un **but**.
Delphine wants to score a goal.

les espadrilles
running shoes

le basketball
basket-bohl
basketball

le golf
golf
golf

le soccer
sok-uhr
soccer

Extra words to learn

l'athlétisme
lat-lay-tee-smah
athletics

le baseball
bayz-bohl
baseball

l'exercice
lek-sair-seess
exercise

le hockey
ok-ay
hockey

le hockey sur gazon
ok-ay sewr gah-so(n)
field hockey

le judo
zhew-do
judo

le karaté
ka-ra-tay
karate

la natation
na-ta-syo(n)
swimming

la plongée
plon-zhay
diving

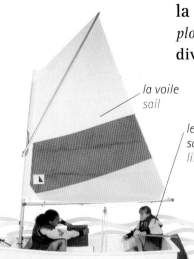

la voile
sail

le gilet de sauvetage
life jacket

faire de la voile
fair duh la vwal
sailing

A imes-tu faire du sport **?**

Je **tire** sur les **rames**.
I'm pulling on the oars.

la rame
oar

la balle
ball

le gant
glove

le bâton
bah-to(n)
bat

faire de l'aviron
fair duh lav-ee-ro(n)
rowing

la raquette
racket

le cheval
horse

le rugby
rewg-bee
rugby

la course à pied
koorss ah pyay
running

l'équitation
lay-keet-a-syo(n)
horseback riding

le tennis
ten-neess
tennis

47

Les animaux familiers

Pets

le chiot
shyoh
puppy

la nourriture
food

Mon chien s'appelle Toby.
My dog's called Toby.

le hamster
am-stair
hamster

Une **tortue bouge** très **lentement.**
A tortoise moves very slowly.

la tortue
tor-tew
tortoise

le cochon d'Inde
ko-sho(n) dand
guinea pig

le lapin
lap-(a)n
rabbit

le collier
collar

le chat
sha
cat

le poisson rouge
pwa-so(n) roozh
goldfish

De quelles couleurs sont les poils du cochon d'Inde **?**

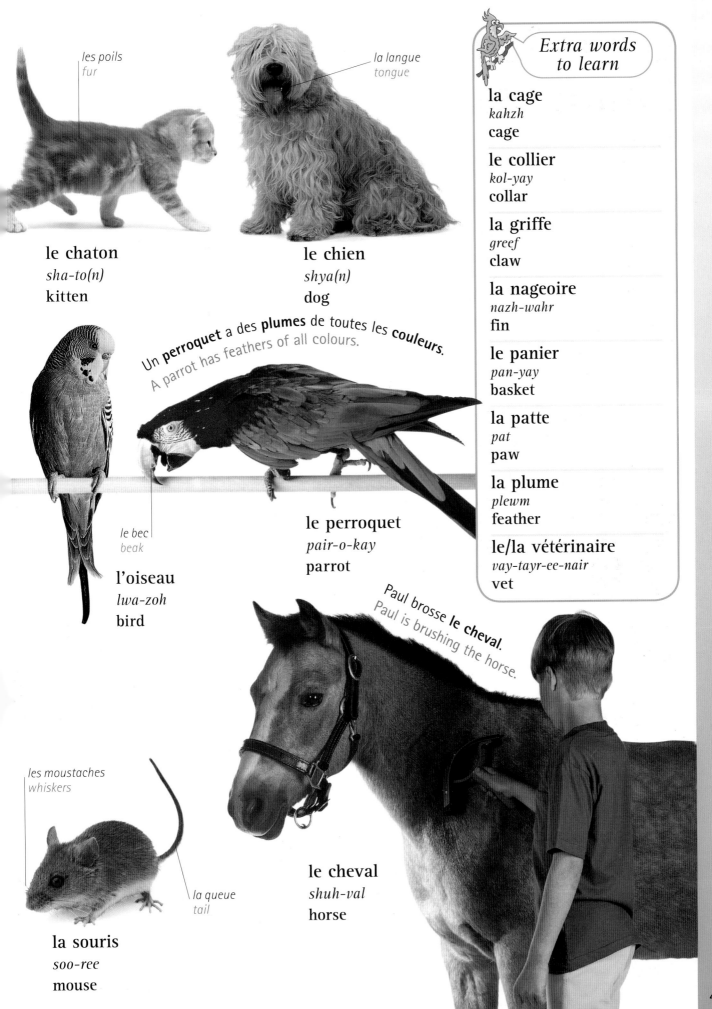

les poils
fur

la langue
tongue

le chaton
sha-to(n)
kitten

le chien
shya(n)
dog

Un **perroquet** a des **plumes** de toutes les **couleurs**.
A parrot has feathers of all colours.

le bec
beak

le perroquet
pair-o-kay
parrot

l'oiseau
lwa-zoh
bird

Paul brosse **le cheval**.
Paul is brushing the horse.

les moustaches
whiskers

la queue
tail

le cheval
shuh-val
horse

la souris
soo-ree
mouse

49

Les couleurs et les formes
Colours and shapes

rouge
roozh
red

orange
or-ahnzh
orange

jaune
zhohn
yellow

vert
vair
green

bleu
bluh
blue

violet
vyo-lay
purple

rose
rohz
pink

brun
bra(n)
brown

noir
nwahr
black

ondulé
wavy

droit
straight

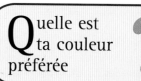

Quelle est ta couleur préférée **?**

le carré
kar-ray
square

le cercle
sair-kluh
circle

l'arc-en-ciel
rainbow

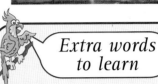

le triangle
tree-yahn-gluh
triangle

l'étoile
lay-twal
star

le losange
lo-zahnzh
diamond

le rectangle
rek-tahn-gluh
rectangle

l'hexagone
ecks-a-gon
hexagon

le pentagone
pahn-ta-gon
pentagon

le cube
kewb
cube

le ballon
bal-o(n)
ball

Les contraires
Opposites

Ouvre grand!
Open wide!

ouvert
oo-vair
open

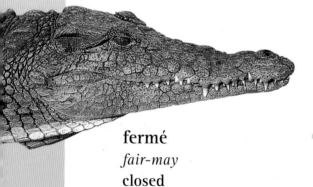

fermé
fair-may
closed

rugueux
rew-ghuh
rough

mouillé
moo-yay
wet

sec
sek
dry

lisse
leess
smooth

sale
sal
dirty

propre
prop-ruh
clean

Extra words to learn

léger
lay-zhay
light (weight)

lent
lah(n)
slow

lourd
loor
heavy

nouveau
noo-voh
new

plein
pla(n)
full

rapide
rap-eed
fast

vide
veed
empty

vieux
vyuh
old

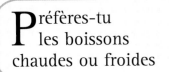

Préfères-tu
les boissons
chaudes ou froides

Une **citrouille** devient **grosse** en **automne**.
A pumpkin gets big in the fall.

froid
frwa
cold

chaud
shoh
hot

gros
groh
fat

Ce **légume** est très **fin**.
This vegetable is very thin.

fin
fa(n)
thin

doux
doo
soft

dur
dewr
hard

Le tournesol a une **grande** tige.
The sunflower has a long stem.

Cette fleur a une **tige courte**.
This flower has a short stem.

court
koor
short

grand
grah(n)
tall

petit
puh-tee
small

grand
grah(n)
big

53

Le temps qu'il fait
Weather

le bonhomme de neige
bon-om duh nehzh
snowman

la neige
nehzh
snow

la tuque
tew-kuh
toque

Il y a beaucoup de vent.
It's very windy.

le parapluie
pa-ra-plwee
umbrella

l'automne
loh-ton
autumn

l'hiver
lee-vair
winter

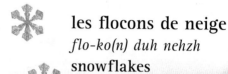

les flocons de neige
flo-ko(n) duh nehzh
snowflakes

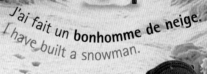

J'ai fait un bonhomme de neige.
I have built a snowman.

Je porte une tuque, un foulard, et des gants.
I'm wearing a toque, scarf, and gloves.

le printemps
pran-tah(m)
spring

l'été
lay-tay
summer

la pluie
plwee
rain

le nuage
new-azh
cloud

le soleil
so-laye
sun

l'arc-en-ciel
lark-ah(n)-syel
rainbow

J'ai un **parapluie** jaune.
I've got a yellow umbrella.

**les lunettes
de soleil**
*lew-net duh
so-laye*
sunglasses

la casquette
kas-ket
cap

Il fait **chaud** au soleil.
It's hot in the sun.

English A–Z

In this section English words are in alphabetical order, followed by the French translation. There is information after each English word to show you what type of word it is. This will help you to make sentences. In French, nouns (naming words) are either masculine or feminine. If the French word has *un* or *le* before it, it is masculine (m), if it has *une* or *la*, it is feminine (f).

(n) = noun (a naming word). Either masculine or feminine. Feminine nouns usually have an "e" at the end.

(adj) = adjective (a describing word). These words can change depending whether the noun they are describing is masculine (m) or feminine (f).

(adv) = adverb (a word that gives more information about a verb, an adjective, or another adverb)

(conj) = conjunction (a joining word, e.g., and)

(prep) = preposition (e.g., about)

(pron) = pronoun (e.g., he, she, it)

(article) = (e.g., a, an, the)

apple
la pomme

a (article)
un/une
a(n)/ewn

about (adv)
environ
ahn-veer-o(n)

about (prep)
sur
sewr

above (prep)
au-dessus de
oh duhs-ew duh

accident (n)
un accident
ak-see-dah(n)

across (prep)
de l'autre côté de
duh loh-truh koh-tay duh

activity (n)
une activité
ak-tee-vee-tay

address (n)
une adresse
a-dress

adult (n)
un/une adulte
ad-ewlt

adventure (n)
une aventure
av-ahn-tewr

after (prep)
après
ap-reh

afternoon (n)
un après-midi
ap-reh mee-dee

again (adv)
encore
ahn-kor

age (n)
l'âge (m)
lahzh

air (n)
l'air (m)
lair

airplane (n)
un avion
av-yo(n)

airport (n)
un aéroport
a-ay-ro-por

alarm clock (n)
un réveil
ray-vaye

all (adj)
tout (m) toute (f)
too/toot

alligator (n)
un alligator
al-ee-gah-tor

almost (adv)
presque
presk

alone (adj)
seul (m) seule (f)
suhl

alphabet (n)
l'alphabet (m)
lal-fa-bay

already (adv)
déjà
day-zha

also (adv)
aussi
oh-see

always (adv)
toujours
too-zhoor

amazing (adj)
incroyable
an-krwa-ya-bluh

ambulance (n)
une ambulance
ahm-bew-lahnss

an (article)
un/une
a(n)/ewn

anchor (n)
une ancre
ahn-kruh

and (conj)
et
eh

angry (adj)
en colère
ah(n) ko-lehr

animal (n)
un animal
an-ee-mal

airplane
l'avion

A
B
C
D
E
F
G
H
I
J
K
L
M
N
O
P
Q
R
S
T
U
V
W
X
Y
Z

ankle (n)
une **cheville**
shuh-vee-ye

answer (n)
une **réponse**
ray-ponss

ant (n)
une **fourmi**
foor-mee

antenna (n)
une **antenne**
ahn-ten

anybody (pron)
n'importe qui
nam-port kee

anything (pron)
n'importe quoi
nam-port kwa

apart (adv)
séparément
say-pa-ray-mah(n)

apartment (n)
un **appartement**
ap-par-tuh-mah(n)

appearance (n)
une **apparence**
ap-par-ahnss

apple (n)
une **pomme**
pom

armchair
le fauteuil

apron (n)
un **tablier**
tab-lee-yay

arch (n)
une **arche**
arsh

area (n)
une **région**
ray-zhyo(n)

arm (n)
un **bras**
bra

armchair (n)
un **fauteuil**
foh-tuh-ye

army (n)
une **armée**
ar-may

around (prep)
autour
oh-toor

arrival (n)
une **arrivée**
ar-ree-vay

arrow (n)
une **flèche**
flehsh

art (n)
l'**art (m)**
lar

astronaut
l'astronaute

artist (n)
un/une **artiste**
ar-teest

assistant (n)
un **assistant**
a-seess-tah(n)
une **assistante**
a-seess-tahnt

astronaut (n)
un/une **astronaute**
astro-noht

astronomer (n)
un/une **astronome**
astro-nom

athletics (n)
l'**athlétisme (m)**
lat-lay-tee-smah

atlas (n)
un **atlas**
at-lahs

attic (n)
un **grenier**
gruhn-yay

aunt (n)
une **tante**
tahnt

autumn (n)
l'**automne (m)**
loh-ton

avocado (n)
un **avocat**
av-o-ka

away (adj)
absent (m)
ap-sah(n)
absente (f)
ap-sahnt

avocado
l'avocat

A
B
C
D
E
F
G
H
I
J
K
L
M
N
O
P
Q
R
S
T
U
V
W
X
Y
Z

B

balloon
le ballon

baboon (n)
un babouin
ba-bwa(n)

baby (n)
un bébé
bay-bay

back (body) (n)
un dos
do

back (adv)
à l'arrière
ah lar-yehr

backpack (n)
un sac à dos
sak ah doh

backwards (adv)
en arrière
ah(n) ar-yehr

bear
l'ours

bad (adj)
mauvais (m)
moh-vay
mauvaise (f)
moh-vayz

badge (n)
un insigne
an-seen-ye

badminton (n)
le badminton
bad-meen-ton

bag (n)
un sac
sak

bakery (n)
une boulangerie
boo-lahn-zhree

balcony (n)
un balcon
bal-ko(n)

ball (n)
un ballon
bal-o(n)
une balle
bal

ballet dancer (n)
un danseur
de ballet
dahn-suhr duh ba-leh
une danseuse
de ballet
dahn-suhz duh ba-leh

balloon (n)
un ballon
bal-o(n)

banana (n)
une banane
ba-nan

band (n)
une bande
bahnd

bank (money) (n)
une banque
bahnk

bank (river) (n)
une rive
reev

barbecue (n)
un barbecue
bar-buhk-yew

barn (n)
une grange
grahnzh

baseball (n)
le baseball
bayz-bohl

basket (n)
un panier
pan-yay

basketball (n)
le basketball
basket-bohl

bat (animal) (n)
une chauve-souris
shohv soo-ree

bat (sports) (n)
un bâton
bah-to(n)

bathing suit (n)
un maillot de bain
ma-yoh duh ba(n)

bathroom (n)
une salle de bains
sal duh ba(n)

bathtub (n)
une baignoire
bayn-wahr

battery (n)
une pile
peel

battle (n)
une bataille
bat-ah-ye

bat
la chauve-souris

beach (n)
une plage
plazh

bead (n)
une perle
pairl

beak (n)
un bec
behk

beans (n)
les haricots (m)
ar-ee-koh

bear (n)
un ours
oorss

beard (n)
une barbe
barb

beautiful (adj)
beau (m) belle (f)
boh/bell

beauty (n)
la beauté
boh-tay

because (conj)
parce que
par-suh-kuh

bed (n)
un lit
lee

bedroom (n)
une chambre
shahm-bruh

bee (n)
une abeille
a-baye

beetle (n)
un scarabée
ska-ra-bay

before (prep)
avant
av-ah(n)

behind (prep)
derrière
dair-yehr

bell (n)
une cloche
klosh

below (prep)
au-dessous de
oh-duh-soo duh

belt (n)
une ceinture
san-tewr

bench (n)
un banc
bah(n)

best (adj)
mieux
myuh

better (adj)
meilleur (m)
meilleure (f)
may-yuhr

binoculars
les jumelles

bike
le vélo

saddle
la selle

pedal
la pédale

tire
le pneu

wheel
la roue

between (prep)
entre
ahn-truh

big (large) (adj)
gros (m) grosse (f)
groh/grohss

big (tall) (adj)
grand (m)
grah(n)
grande (f)
grahnd

bike (n)
un vélo
vay-lo

bill (n)
une facture
fak-tuh-ruh

billion
un milliard
meel-yar

binoculars (n)
les jumelles (f)
zhew-mel

bird (n)
un oiseau
wa-zoh

birthday (n)
un anniversaire
an-ee-vair-sair

birthday cake (n)
un gâteau
d'anniversaire
gah-toh dan-ee-vair-sair

birthday card (n)
une carte
d'anniversaire
kart dan-ee-vair-sair

black (adj)
noir (m) noire (f)
nwahr

blackboard (n)
un tableau noir
tab-loh nwahr

blanket (n)
une couverture
koo-vair-tewr

blonde (adj)
blond (m)
bloh(n)
blonde (f)
blohnd

blood (n)
le sang
sah(n)

blouse (n)
un chemisier
shuh-meez-yay

blue (adj)
bleu (m) bleue (f)
bluh

board (notice) (n)
un panneau
pan-noh

board game (n)
un jeu de plateau
zhuh duh pla-toh

boat (n)
un bateau
ba-toh

A
(B)
C
D
E
F
G
H
I
J
K
L
M
N
O
P
Q
R
S
T
U
V
W
X
Y
Z

body (n)
un **corps**
kor

bone (n)
un **os**
oss

book (n)
un **livre**
leev-ruh

bookstore (n)
une **librairie**
leeb-rair-ee

boot (n)
une **botte**
bot

boring (adj)
ennuyeux (m)
ahn-wee-yuh
ennuyeuse (f)
ahn-wee-yuhz

bottle (n)
une **bouteille**
boo-taye

bottom (n)
le **fond**
foh(n)

bowl (cereal) (n)
un **bol**
bol

box (n)
une **boîte**
bwat

boy (n)
un **garçon**
gar-so(n)

boyfriend (n)
un **petit ami**
puh-tee-ta-mee

bracelet (n)
un **bracelet**
bra-slay

brain (n)
un **cerveau**
sair-voh

branch (n)
une **branche**
brahnsh

brave (adj)
courageux (m)
koor-a-zhuh
courageuse (f)
koor-a-zhuhz

bread (n)
un **pain**
pa(n)

break (n)
une **pause**
pohz

breakfast (n)
un **petit-déjeuner**
puh-tee day-zhuh-nay

breeze (n)
une **brise**
breez

butterfly
le papillon

bridge (n)
un **pont**
po(n)

bright (adj)
brillant (m)
bree-yah(n)
brillante (f)
bree-yahnt

broken (adj)
cassé (m) **cassée** (f)
kah-say

broom (n)
un **balai**
ba-lay

brother (n)
un **frère**
frair

brown (adj)
brun
bra(n)

bubble (n)
une **bulle**
bewl

bucket (n)
un **seau**
soh

building (n)
un **bâtiment**
bah-tee-mah(n)

bulb (light) (n)
une **ampoule**
ahm-pool

bubbles
les bulles

bulb (plant) (n)
un **bulbe**
bewlb

buoy (n)
une **bouée**
boo-way

bus (n)
un **autobus**
ohto-bews

bus stop (n)
un **arrêt d'autobus**
ar-reh dohto-bews

bush (n)
un **buisson**
bwee-so(n)

business (n)
les **affaires**
a-fair

busy (adj)
occupé (m)
occupée (f)
ok-ew-pay

but (conj)
mais
may

butter (n)
le **beurre**
buhr

butterfly (n)
un **papillon**
pa-pee-yo(n)

button (n)
un **bouton**
boo-to(n)

C

cake
le gâteau

cabbage (n)
un chou
shoo

café (n)
un café
ka-fay

cage (n)
une cage
kahzh

cake (n)
un gâteau
gah-toh

calculator (n)
une calculatrice
kal-kew-la-treess

calendar (n)
un calendrier
kal-ahn-dree-yay

calf (n)
un veau
voh

calm (adj)
calme
kalm

camel (n)
un chameau
sha-moh

camera (n)
un appareil photo
ap-pa-ray fo-toh

can (n)
un bidon
bee-do(n)

candle (n)
une bougie
boo-zhee

candy (n)
un bonbon
bo(n)-bo(n)

canoe (n)
un canoé
kan-o-ay

cap (n)
une casquette
kas-ket

capital (n)
une capitale
ka-pee-tal

car (n)
une voiture
vwah-tewr

card (n)
une carte
kart

cardboard (n)
le carton
kar-to(n)

cards (n)
les cartes (f)
kart

careful (adj)
prudent (m)
prew-dah(n)
prudente (f)
prew-dahnt

carousel (n)
un tourniquet
toor-nee-kay

carpet (n)
une moquette
moh-ket

carrot (n)
une carotte
ka-rot

cart (n)
une charrette
sha-ret

cart (shopping) (n)
un chariot
shar-yoh

cash (n)
en espèces
ah(n) es-pehss

cat (n)
un chat
sha

caterpillar (n)
une chenille
shuh-nee-ye

cave (n)
une grotte
grot

CD (n)
un CD
say-day

CD player (n)
un lecteur de CD
lek-tuhr duh say-day

ceiling (n)
un plafond
pla-fo(n)

cellar (n)
une cave
kav

cellphone (n)
un téléphone cellulaire
tay-lay-fon sel-luh-lare

centre (n)
le centre
sahn-truh

cereal (n)
une céréale
sair-ay-al

certain (adj)
certain (m)
sair-ta(n)
certaine (f)
sair-tehn

chain (n)
une chaîne
shehn

chair (n)
une chaise
shehz

challenge (n)
un défi
day-fee

change (n)
un changement
shahnzh-mah(n)

car
la voiture

window
la fenêtre

door
la porte

A
B
C
D
E
F
G
H
I
J
K
L
M
N
O
P
Q
R
S
T
U
V
W
X
Y
Z

A
B
C
D
E
F
G
H
I
J
K
L
M
N
O
P
Q
R
S
T
U
V
W
X
Y
Z

cheap (adj)
bon marché
bo(n) mar-shay

checkout (n)
une caisse
kehss

cheese (n)
un fromage
fro-mazh

cheetah (n)
un guépard
gay-par

chef (n)
un/une chef
shef

chess (n)
les échecs (m)
ay-shek

chest (n)
une poitrine
pwa-treen

**chest of
drawers (n)**
une commode
kom-mod

chewing gum (n)
une gomme
à macher
gom a mah-shay

cheese
le fromage

chick (n)
un poussin
poo-sa(n)

chicken (n)
un poulet
poo-lay

child (n)
un/une enfant
ahn-fah(n)

children (n)
les enfants
ahn-fah(n)

chimney (n)
une cheminée
shuh-mee-nay

chimpanzee (n)
un chimpanzé
shahm-pahn-zay

chin (n)
un menton
mahn-to(n)

chocolate (n)
le chocolat
sho-ko-la

Christmas (n)
Noël
no-el

church (n)
une église
ayg-leess

circle (n)
un cercle
sair-kluh

circus (n)
un cirque
seerk

city (n)
une ville
veel

classroom (n)
une salle de classe
sal duh klahss

claw (n)
une griffe
greef

clean (adj)
propre
prop-ruh

clear (adj)
clair (m) claire (f)
klair

clever (adj)
intelligent (m)
an-tel-lee-zhah(n)
intelligente (f)
an-tel-lee-zhahnt

cliff (n)
une falaise
fa-lehz

cloak (n)
une cape
kap

clock (n)
une horloge
or-lozh

close (near) (adj)
proche
prosh

closed (adj)
fermé (m) fermée (f)
fair-may

cloth (n)
un tissu
tee-soo

clothes (n)
les vêtements
veht-mah(n)

cloud (n)
un nuage
new-azh

cloudy (adj)
nuageux (m)
new-azh-uh
nuageuse (f)
new-azh-uhz

clown (n)
un clown
kloon

coach (n)
un autocar
ohto-kar

coast (n)
une côte
koht

coat (n)
un manteau
mahn-toh

coat hanger (n)
un cintre
san-truh

coffee (n)
le café
ka-fay

coin (n)
une pièce
de monnaie
pyehs duh mon-neh

cold (adj)
froid (m)
frwa
froide (f)
frwad

collar (n)
un collier
kol-yay

colour (n)
une couleur
koo-luhr

compass
la boussole

coloured pencil (n)
un **crayon de couleur**
kra-yo(n) duh koo-luhr

colourful (adj)
coloré (m)
colorée (f)
ko-lo-ray

comb (n)
un **peigne**
pain-ye

combine harvester (n)
une **moissonneuse-batteuse**
mwa-son-nuhz bat-tuhz

comfortable (adj)
confortable
kon-for-ta-bluh

comic (n)
un **comique**
ko-meek

compass (n)
une **boussole**
boo-sol

crab
le crabe

computer (n)
un **ordinateur**
or-dee-na-tuhr

computer game (n)
un **jeu électronique**
zhuh ay-lek-tro-neek

concert (n)
un **concert**
kon-sair

continent (n)
un **continent**
kon-tee-nah(n)

controls (n)
les **commandes** (f)
ko-mahnd

cookie (n)
un **biscuit**
bee-skwee

cool (adj)
frais (m)
fray
fraîche (f)
frehsh

corner (n)
un **coin**
kwa(n)

correct (adj)
juste
zhewst

costume (n)
un **déguisement**
day-gheez-mah(n)

cotton (n)
le **coton**
ko-to(n)

cough (n)
une **toux**
too

country (n)
un **pays**
pay-ee

countryside (n)
la **campagne**
kahm-pan-ye

cousin (n)
un **cousin**
koo-za(n)
une **cousine**
koo-zeen

cow (n)
une **vache**
vash

cowboy (n)
un **cow-boy**
koh-boye

crab (n)
un **crabe**
krab

crane (n)
une **grue**
grew

crayon (n)
un **crayon de cire**
kray-yo(n) duh seer

cream (n)
la **crème**
krehm

creature (n)
une **bête**
beht

crew (n)
un **équipage**
ay-kee-pazh

crocodile (n)
un **crocodile**
kro-ko-deel

crop (n)
une **récolte**
ray-kolt

crossing (n)
un **carrefour**
kar-foor

crowded (adj)
bondé (m)
bondée (f)
bon-day

crown (n)
une **couronne**
koo-ron

cube (n)
un **cube**
kewb

cup (n)
une **tasse**
tahss

cupboard (n)
un **placard**
pla-kar

curious (adj)
curieux (m)
kew-ree-uh
curieuse (f)
kew-ree-uhz

curly (adj)
frisé (m) frisée (f)
free-zay

curtain (n)
un **rideau**
ree-doh

curved (adj)
courbe
koorb

cushion (n)
un **coussin**
koo-sa(n)

customer (n)
un **client**
klee-ah(n)
une **cliente**
klee-ahnt

crown
la couronne

A
B
C
D
E
F
G
H
I
J
K
L
M
N
O
P
Q
R
S
T
U
V
W
X
Y
Z

A
B
C
D
E
F
G
H
I
J
K
L
M
N
O
P
Q
R
S
T
U
V
W
X
Y
Z

D

daisy
la marguerite

dad (n)
papa
pa-pa

dairy (adj)
laitier (m) laitière (f)
layt-yay/layt-yair

daisy (n)
une marguerite
mahr-guh-reet

dancer (n)
un danseur
dahn-suhr
une danseuse
dahn-suhz

dandelion (n)
un pissenlit
pee-sahn-lee

danger (n)
un danger
dahn-zhay

dangerous (adj)
dangereux (m)
dahn-zhay-ruh
dangereuse (f)
dahn-zhay-ruhz

dark (adj)
sombre
som-bruh

date (n)
une date
dat

daughter (n)
une fille
fee-ye

day (n)
un jour
zhoor

dead (adj)
mort (m) morte (f)
mor/mort

deaf (adj)
sourd (m) sourde (f)
soor/soord

dear (adj)
cher (m) chère (f)
shair

deck (boat) (n)
un pont
po(n)

deck chair (n)
une chaise longue
shayz long-uh

decoration (n)
une décoration
day-ko-ra-syo(n)

deep (adj)
profond (m)
pro-fo(n)
profonde (f)
pro-fond

deer (n)
un chevreuil
shuh-vruh-ye

delicious (adj)
délicieux (m)
day-lee-syuh
délicieuse (f)
day-lee-syuhz

dentist (n)
un/une dentiste
dahn-teest

desert (n)
un désert
day-zair

desk (n)
un bureau
bew-roh

dessert (n)
un dessert
duh-sair

diagram (n)
un diagramme
dya-gram

diamond (shape) (n)
un losange
lo-zahnzh

diary (n)
un journal
zhoor-nal

dice (n)
les dés
day

dictionary (n)
un dictionnaire
deek-syo-nair

different (adj)
différent (m)
dee-fay-rah(n)
différente (f)
dee-fay-rahnt

difficult (adj)
difficile
dee-fee-seel

digital (adj)
digital (m)
digitale (f)
dee-zhee-tal

dining room (n)
une salle à manger
sal ah mahn-zhay

dinner (n)
un dîner
dee-nay

dinosaur (n)
un dinosaure
dee-noh-zor

direction (n)
une direction
dee-rek-syo(n)

directly (adv)
directement
dee-rek-tuh-mah(n)

dirty (adj)
sale
sal

disabled (adj)
handicapé (m)
handicapée (f)
ahn-dee-ka-pay

dish towel (n)
un torchon
tor-sho(n)

distance (n)
une distance
dee-stahnss

diving (n)
la plongée
plon-zhay

divorced (adj)
divorcé (m)
divorcée (f)
dee-vor-say

doctor (n)
un médecin
may-duh-sa(n)

dog (n)
un chien
shya(n)

doll (n)
une poupée
poo-pay

dolphin (n)
un dauphin
doh-fa(n)

dome (n)
un dôme
dohm

door (n)
une porte
port

downstairs (adv)
en bas
ah(n) bah

dragon (n)
un dragon
dra-go(n)

dragonfly (n)
une libellule
lee-bel-lewl

drawer (n)
un tiroir
teer-wahr

drawing (act of) (n)
le dessin
de-sa(n)

dream (n)
un rêve
rehv

dress (n)
une robe
rob

drink (n)
une boisson
bwa-so(n)

drinking straw (n)
une paille
pah-ye

drop (n)
une goutte
goot

drugstore (n)
une pharmacie
far-ma-see

drum (n)
un tambour
tahm-boor

drum kit (n)
une batterie
bat-tree

dry (adj)
sec (m) sèche (f)
sek/sehsh

duck (n)
un canard
ka-nar

duckling (n)
un caneton
ka-nuh-to(n)

during (prep)
pendant
pahn-dah(n)

dust (n)
la poussière
poo-syair

duvet (n)
une couette
koo-et

DVD (n)
un DVD
day-vay-day

DVD player (n)
un lecteur de DVD
lek-tuhr duh day-vay-day

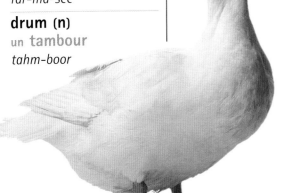

duck
le canard

E

egg
l'œuf

each (adj)
chaque
shak

eagle (n)
un aigle
ay-gluh

ear (n)
une oreille
o-raye

earache (n)
un mal d'oreille
mal do-raye

early (adv)
tôt
toh

earring (n)
une boucle
d'oreille
book-luh do-raye

Earth (planet) (n)
la Terre
tair

earthworm (n)
un ver de terre
vair duh tair

east (n)
l'est (m)
lest

easy (adj)
facile
fa-seel

echo (n)
un écho
ay-ko

edge (n)
le bord
bor

effect (n)
un effet
ay-fay

egg (n)
un œuf
uhf

elbow (n)
un coude
kood

electrical (adj)
électrique
ay-lek-treek

elephant (n)
un éléphant
ay-lay-fah(n)

elevator (n)
un ascenseur
a-sahn-suhr

email (n)
un courriel
koo-ree-yel

email address (n)
une adresse
électronique
a-dress ay-lek-tro-neek

emergency (n)
une urgence
ewr-zhahnss

empty (adj)
vide
veed

encyclopedia (n)
une encyclopédie
ahn-see-klo-pay-dee

A
B
C
(D)
(E)
F
G
H
I
J
K
L
M
N
O
P
Q
R
S
T
U
V
W
X
Y
Z

A
B
C
D
(E)
F
G
H
I
J
K
L
M
N
O
P
Q
R
S
T
U
V
W
X
Y
Z

end (final part) (n)
la **fin**
fa(n)

English (n)
l'**anglais** (m)
lahn-glay

enough (adj)
assez
a-say

enthusiastic (adj)
enthousiaste
ahn-too-zee-ast

entrance (n)
une **entrée**
ahn-tray

envelope (n)
une **enveloppe**
ahn-vlop

environment (n)
un **environnement**
ahn-vee-ron-mah(n)

equal (adj)
égal (m) **égale** (f)
ay-gal

equator (n)
l'**équateur** (m)
lay-kwa-tuhr

equipment (n)
le **matériel**
ma-tay-ree-el

eraser (n)
une **gomme à effacer**
gom ah eh-fas-say

even (adv)
même
mehm

exercise
l'exercice

envelope
l'enveloppe

Banque Nationale
123 Blvd. des Chutes
Montréal, Québec
H4A 2B8

stamp
le timbre

address
l'adresse

evening (n)
un **soir**
swahr

event (n)
un **événement**
ay-vayn-mah(n)

every (adj)
tous
too

everybody (pron)
tout le monde
too luh mond

everyday (adv)
tous les jours
too lay zhoor

everything (pron)
tout
too

everywhere (adv)
partout
par-too

exam (n)
un **examen**
eg-za-ma(n)

excellent (adj)
excellent (m)
ek-say-lah(n)
excellente (f)
ek-say-lahnt

exchange (n)
un **échange**
ay-shahnzh

excited (adj)
excité (m)
excitée (f)
ek-see-tay

exercise (n)
un **exercice**
ek-sair-seess

exercise book (n)
un **cahier**
ka-yay

exit (n)
la **sortie**
sor-tee

expedition (n)
une **expédition**
ek-spay-dee-syo(n)

expensive (adj)
cher (m) **chère** (f)
shair

experiment (n)
une **expérience**
ek-spay-ree-ahnss

expert (n)
un **expert**
ek-spair
une **experte**
ek-spairt

explorer (n)
un **explorateur**
ek-splor-a-tuhr
une **exploratrice**
ek-splor-a-treess

explosion (n)
une **explosion**
ek-sploh-zyo(n)

extinct (adj)
disparu (m)
dees-pah-rew
disparue (f)
dees-pah-rew

extra (adj)
supplémentaire
soo-play-mahn-tair

extremely (adv)
extrêmement
ek-streh-muh-mah(n)

eye (n)
un **œil**
uh-ye

eyebrow (n)
un **sourcil**
soor-seel

eyelash (n)
un **cil**
seel

arm
le bras

leg
la jambe

hand
la main

foot
le pied

F

fashion
la mode

fabulous (adj)
fabuleux (m)
fa-bew-luh
fabuleuse (f)
fa-bew-luhz

face (n)
un visage
vee-zazh

facecloth (n)
une débarbouillette
day-bar-boo-yet

fact (n)
un fait
fay

factory (n)
une usine
ew-zeen

faint (pale) (adj)
faible
fay-bluh

fair (n)
une foire
fwahr

fairground (n)
un parc d'attractions
park dah-track-syo(n)

false (adj)
faux (m) fausse (f)
foh/fohss

family (n)
une famille
fa-mee-ye

famous (adj)
célèbre
say-lay-bruh

fantastic (adj)
fantastique
fan-tas-teek

far (adv)
loin
lwa(n)

farm (n)
une ferme
fairm

farmer (n)
un fermier
fairm-yay
une fermière
fairm-yair

fashion (n)
la mode
mod

fashionable (adj)
à la mode
ah la mod

fast (adv)
rapide
rap-eed

fat (adj)
gros (m) grosse (f)
groh/grohss

father (n)
un père
pair

favourite (adj)
préféré (m)
préférée (f)
pray-fair-ay

feather (n)
une plume
plewm

felt-tip pen (n)
un feutre
fuh-truh

female (human) (n)
une femme
fam

fence (n)
une clôture
kloh-tew-ruh

ferry (n)
un traversier
tra-vehr-syah

festival (n)
une fête
feht

field (n)
un champ
shah(m)

field hockey (n)
le hockey
sur gazon
ok-ay soor gah-zo(n)

film (n)
un film
feelm

film star (n)
une vedette
de cinéma
vuh-det duh see-nay-ma

fin (n)
une nageoire
nazh-wahr

fine (adv)
bien
bya(n)

finger (n)
un doigt
dwa

fire (n)
un feu
fuh

fire engine (n)
un camion
de pompier
kam-yo(n) duh pomp-yay

firefighter (n)
un pompier
pomp-yay

first (adv)
d'abord
da-bor

first (adj)
premier (m)
pruhm-yay
première (f)
pruhm-yair

first aid (n)
les premiers
soins (m)
pruhm-yay swa(n)

fish (n)
un poisson
pwa-so(n)

fishing (n)
la pêche
pehsh

fishing boat (n)
un bateau de pêche
ba-toh duh pehsh

fish
le poisson

fin
la nageoire

eye
l'œil

A B C D E **F** G H I J K L M N O P Q R S T U V W X Y Z

A
B
C
D
E
(F)
G
H
I
J
K
L
M
N
O
P
Q
R
S
T
U
V
W
X
Y
Z

Canadian flag
le drapeau canadien

fit (adj)
en forme
ah(n) form

flag (n)
un **drapeau**
dra-poh

flashlight (n)
une **lampe de poche**
lahmp duh posh

flat (adj)
plat (m) **plate** (f)
pla/plat

fleece (n)
un **polar**
po-lar

flipper (n)
une **palme**
palm

flock (of sheep) (n)
un **troupeau**
troo-poh

flood (n)
une **inondation**
in-on-da-syo(n)

floor (n)
le **sol**
sol

flour (n)
la **farine**
far-een

flower (n)
une **fleur**
fluhr

flute (n)
une **flûte**
flewt

fly (n)
une **mouche**
moosh

fog (n)
le **brouillard**
broo-yar

food (n)
la **nourriture**
noo-ree-tewr

foot (human) (n)
un **pied**
pyay

foot (animal) (n)
une **patte**
pat

foreign (adj)
étranger (m)
ay-trahn-zhay
étrangère (f)
ay-trahn-zhair

forest (n)
une **forêt**
fo-reh

fork (n)
une **fourchette**
foor-shet

forward (adv)
en **avant**
ah(n) av-ah(n)

fox (n)
un **renard**
ruh-nar

frame (n)
un **cadre**
kah-druh

free (no cost) (adj)
gratuit (m) **gratuite** (f)
gra-twee/gra-tweet

free (not confined) (adj)
libre
lee-bruh

free time (n)
le **temps libre**
tah(n) lee-bruh

freedom (n)
la **liberté**
lee-bair-tay

freezer (n)
un **congélateur**
kon-zhay-la-tuhr

French (n)
le **français**
frahn-say

fresh (adj)
frais (m) **fraîche** (f)
fray/frehsh

fridge (n)
un **réfrigérateur**
ray-free-zhair-a-tuhr

friend (n)
un **ami**, une **amie**
a-mee

friendly (adj)
amical (m)
amicale (f)
a-mee-kal

fries (n)
les **frites** (f)
freet

frightened (adj)
effrayé (m)
effrayée (f)
eh-fray-yay

frog (n)
une **grenouille**
gruh-noo-ye

from (prep)
de
duh

front door (n)
une **porte d'entrée**
port dahn-tray

frozen (adj)
gelé (m) **gelée** (f)
zhuh-lay

fruit (n)
un **fruit**
frwee

frying pan (n)
une **poêle**
pwal

fuel (n)
le **carburant**
kar-bew-rah(n)

full (adj)
plein (m) **pleine** (f)
pla(n)/plen

fun (n)
un **amusement**
am-ewz-mah(n)

fun (adj)
amusant (m)
amusante (f)
*ah-muz-ah(n)/
ah-muz-ah(n)t*

fur (n)
les **poils** (m)
pwal

furniture (n)
les **meubles** (m)
muh-bluh

future (n)
l'**avenir** (m)
lav-neer

frog
la grenouille

globe
le globe

game (n)
un jeu
zhuh

garage (n)
un garage
gar-azh

garbage (n)
les ordures (f)
or-dewr

garbage can (n)
une poubelle
poo-bell

garden (n)
un jardin
zhar-da(n)

gardener (n)
un jardinier
zhar-deen-yay
une jardinière
zhar-deen-yair

gardening (n)
le jardinage
zhar-dee-nazh

gas (n)
le gaz
gahz

gas (fuel) (n)
l'essence (f)
le-sahns

gentle (adj)
doux (m) douce (f)
doo/dooss

giant (n)
un géant
zhay-ah(n)

gift (n)
un cadeau
ka-doh

giraffe (n)
une girafe
zhee-raf

girl (n)
une fille
fee-ye

girlfriend (n)
une petite amie
puh-teet a-mee

glass (drink) (n)
un verre
vair

glasses (n)
les lunettes (f)
lew-net

globe (n)
un globe
glob

glove (n)
un gant
gah(n)

glue (n)
la colle
kol

goal (n)
un but
bewt

goat (n)
une chèvre
shay-vruh

God (n)
Dieu
dyuh

gold (n)
l'or (m)
lor

goldfish (n)
un poisson rouge
pwa-so(n) roozh

golf (n)
le golf
golf

good (adj)
bon (m) bonne (f)
bo(n)/bon

gorilla (n)
un gorille
go-ree-ye

government (n)
un gouvernement
goo-vairn-mah(n)

grandfather (n)
un grand-père
grah(n)-pair

grandmother (n)
une grand-mère
grah(n)-mair

grandparents (n)
les grands-parents
grah(n)-par-ah(n)

grape (n)
le raisin
ray-za(n)

grass (n)
l'herbe (f)
lairb

grasshopper (n)
une sauterelle
soht-rel

great (adj)
formidable
for-mee-da-bluh

green (adj)
vert (m) verte (f)
vair/vairt

greenhouse (n)
une serre
sair

ground (n)
la terre
tair

group (n)
un groupe
groop

guide (n)
un guide
gheed

guinea pig (n)
un cochon d'Inde
ko-sho(n) dand

guitar (n)
une guitare
ghee-tar

gymnastics (n)
la gymnastique
zheem-nas-teek

guitar
la guitare

A
B
C
D
E
F
G
H
I
J
K
L
M
N
O
P
Q
R
S
T
U
V
W
X
Y
Z

69

hot-air balloon
la montgolfière

habit (n)
l'habitude (f)
lab-ee-tude

habitat (n)
un habitat
a-bee-ta

hair (n)
les cheveux
shuh-vuh

hairbrush (n)
une brosse
à cheveux
bros ah shuh-vuh

hairdresser (n)
un coiffeur
kwa-fuhr
une coiffeuse
kwa-fuhz

hairy (adj)
poilu (m) poilue (f)
pwa-lew

half (n)
une moitié
mwat-yay

hall (n)
un couloir
kool-wahr

hamster (n)
un hamster
am-stair

hand (n)
une main
ma(n)

handkerchief (n)
un mouchoir
moosh-wahr

handsome (adj)
beau (m)
boh
belle (f)
bell

hang-glider (n)
un deltaplane
delta-plan

happy (adj)
content (m)
kon-tah(n)
contente (f)
kon-tahnt

harbour (n)
un port
por

hard (adj)
dur (m) dure (f)
dewr

hard drive (n)
un disque dur
deesk dewr

hare (n)
un lièvre
lyeh-vruh

harvest (n)
une moisson
mwa-so(n)

hat (n)
un chapeau
sha-poh

hawk (n)
un faucon
foh-ko(n)

hay (n)
le foin
fwa(n)

he (pron)
il
eel

head (n)
une tête
teht

headache (n)
un mal de tête
mal duh teht

headphones (n)
les écouteurs (m)
eh-koo-tuhr

healthy (adj)
en bonne santé
ah(n) bon sahn-tay

heart (n)
un cœur
kuhr

heat (n)
la chaleur
sha-luhr

heavy (adj)
lourd (m) lourde (f)
loor/loord

helicopter (n)
un hélicoptère
ay-lee-kop-tair

helmet (n)
un casque
kask

help (n)
une aide
ehd

her/his (adj)
son (m) sa (f)
so(n)/sa

her/him (pron)
la (her)
le (him)
l' (before a vowel)
la/luh/l

hamster
le hamster

hero (n)
un héros (m)
air-o
un héroine (f)
air-o-a(n)

heron (n)
un héron
air-o(n)

hers/his (pron)
le sien (m)
luh sya(n)
la sienne (f)
la syen

hexagon (n)
un hexagone
ecks-a-gon

hi
salut
sa-lew

hide-and-seek (n)
cache-cache
kash-kash

high (adj)
haut (m) haute (f)
oh/oht

highway (n)
une autoroute
oh-toh-root

hill (n)
une colline
kol-leen

hip (n)
une **hanche**
ahnsh

historical (adj)
historique
ee-stor-eek

history (n)
l'histoire (f)
leest-wahr

hive (n)
une **ruche**
rewsh

hobby (n)
un **passe-temps**
pass-ta(n)

hockey (n)
le **hockey**
ok-ay

hole (n)
un **trou**
troo

holiday (n)
les **vacances** (f)
vak-ahnss

home (n)
la **maison**
may-zo(n)

homework (n)
les **devoirs** (m)
duhv-wahr

honey (n)
le **miel**
myel

hood (n)
un **capuchon** (n)
kap-ewsh-o(n)

horn (n)
une **corne**
korn

horrible (adj)
horrible
o-ree-bluh

horse (n)
un **cheval**
shuh-val

horseback riding (n)
l'équitation (f)
lay-keet-a-syo(n)

hospital (n)
un **hôpital**
o-pee-tal

hot (adj)
chaud (m)
shoh
chaude (f)
shohd

hot-air balloon (n)
une **montgolfière**
mohn-golf-yair

hot chocolate (n)
un **chocolat chaud**
sho-ko-la shoh

hot dog (n)
un **hot-dog**
ot-dog

hotel (n)
un **hôtel**
o-tel

hour (n)
l'heure (f)
luhr

house (n)
une **maison**
may-zo(n)

how (adv)
comment
ko-mah(n)

huge (adj)
énorme
ay-norm

human (n)
un **être humain**
eh-truh ew-ma(n)

hummingbird (n)
un **oiseau-mouche**
wa-zoh-moosh

honey
le miel

hungry (adj)
affamé (m)
affamée (f)
af-fa-may

hurricane (n)
un **ouragan**
oo-ra-gah(n)

husband (n)
un **mari**
ma-ree

hut (n)
une **cabane**
ka-ban

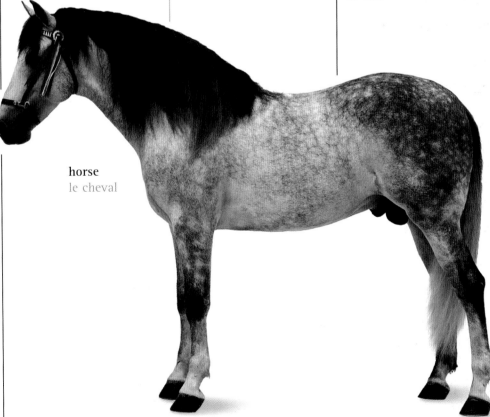

horse
le cheval

A
B
C
D
E
F
G
(H)
I
J
K
L
M
N
O
P
Q
R
S
T
U
V
W
X
Y
Z

A
B
C
D
E
F
G
H
(I)
J
K
L
M
N
O
P
Q
R
S
T
U
V
W
X
Y
Z

island
l'île

I (pron)
je/j'
zhuh/zh

ice (n)
la glace
glass

ice cream (n)
une crème glacée
krehm glasay

ice cube (n)
un glaçon
glass-o(n)

ice cream
la crème glacée

ice skating (n)
le patinage
sur glace
pa-tee-nazh sewr glass

idea (n)
une idée
ee-day

ill (adj)
malade
ma-lad

illness (n)
une maladie
ma-la-dee

illustration (n)
une illustration
eel-lew-stra-syo(n)

immediately (adv)
tout de suite
too duh sweet

important (adj)
important (m)
am-por-tah(n)
importante (f)
am-por-tahnt

impossible (adj)
impossible
am-po-see-bluh

information (n)
une information
an-for-ma-syo(n)

ingredient (n)
un ingrédient
an-gray-diah(n)

injury (n)
une blessure
bless-ewr

ink (n)
l'encre (f)
lahn-kruh

insect (n)
un insecte
an-sekt

inside (prep)
à l'intérieur de
ah lan-tayr-yuhr duh

instruction (n)
une instruction
an-strewk-syo(n)

instrument (n)
un instrument
an-strew-mah(n)

interesting (adj)
intéressant (m)
an-tair-ay-sah(n)
intéressante (f)
an-tair-ay-sahnt

international (adj)
international (m)
internationale (f)
an-tair-na-syo-nal

Internet (n)
Internet (m)
lin-tair-net

into (prep)
dans
dah(n)

introduction (n)
une présentation
pray-zahn-ta-syon(n)

invitation (n)
une invitation
an-vee-ta-syo(n)

iron (clothes) (n)
un fer à repasser
fair ah ruh-pah-say

island (n)
une île
eel

its (adj)
son (m) sa (f)
so(n)/sa

it's (it is)
c'est
say

ice skating
le patinage sur glace

dress
la robe

leg
la jambe

J

jug
la cruche

jacket (n)
un **blouson**
bloo-zo(n)

jam (n)
la **confiture**
kon-fee-tewr

jeans (n)
un **jean**
jeen

jellyfish (n)
une **méduse**
may-dewz

jet (n)
un **avion à réaction**
av-yo(n) ah ray-ak-syo(n)

jewel (n)
un **bijou**
bee-zhoo

jewellery (n)
les **bijoux**
bee-zhoo

job (n)
un **emploi**
am-plwa

joke (n)
une **blague**
blag

journey (n)
un **voyage**
vwa-yazh

judo (n)
le **judo**
zhew-doh

jug (n)
une **cruche**
krewsh

juice (n)
le **jus**
zhew

jungle (n)
la **jungle**
zhahn-gluh

just (adv)
juste
zhewst

jeans
le jean

K

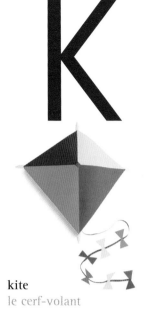

kite
le cerf-volant

kangaroo (n)
un **kangourou**
kahn-goo-roo

karate (n)
le **karaté**
ka-ra-tay

kettle (n)
une **bouilloire**
booy-wahr

key (n)
une **clé**
klay

keyboard (n)
un **clavier**
klav-yay

kind (gentle) (adj)
gentil (m)
zhahn-tee
gentille (f)
zhahn-teeye

kind (type) (n)
une **sorte**
sort

king (n)
un **roi**
rwa

kiss (n)
un **baiser**
bay-zay

kitchen (n)
une **cuisine**
kwee-zeen

kite (n)
un **cerf-volant**
sair-vo-lah(n)

kitten (n)
un **chaton**
sha-to(n)

knee (n)
un **genou**
zhuh-noo

knife (n)
un **couteau**
koo-toh

knight (n)
un **chevalier**
shuh-val-yay

knot (n)
un **nœud**
nuh

koala (n)
un **koala**
ko-a-la

kitten
le chaton

tail
la queue

A B C D E F G H I J K L M N O P Q R S T U V W X Y Z

73

A
B
C
D
E
F
G
H
I
J
K
(L)
M
N
O
P
Q
R
S
T
U
V
W
X
Y
Z

L

lemon
le citron

ladder (n)
une **échelle**
ay-shell

ladybug (n)
une **coccinelle**
kok-see-nel

lake (n)
un **lac**
lak

lamb (n)
un **agneau**
an-yoh

lamp (n)
une **lampe**
lahmp

land (n)
un **terrain**
tair-ra(n)

language (n)
une **langue**
lahn-guh

laptop (n)
un **ordinateur**
portable
or-dee-na-tuhr
por-ta-bluh

last (adj)
dernier (m)
dairn-yay
dernière (f)
dairn-yair

late (adv)
en retard
ah(n) ruh-tar

law (n)
une **loi**
lwa

lawn (n)
une **pelouse**
puh-looz

lawn mower (n)
une **tondeuse**
à gazon
ton-duhz ah gah-zo(n)

lazy (adj)
paresseux (m)
pa-re-suh
paresseuse (f)
pa-re-suhz

leaf (n)
une **feuille**
fuh-ye

leather (adj)
en cuir
ah(n) kweer

left (adj)
gauche
gohsh

left-handed (adj)
gaucher (m)
goh-shay
gauchère (f)
goh-shair

leg (n)
une **jambe**
zhahmb

lemon (n)
un **citron**
see-tro(n)

lemonade (n)
une **limonade**
lee-mon-ad

leopard (n)
un **léopard**
lay-o-par

lesson (n)
une **leçon**
le-so(n)

letter (n)
une **lettre**
let-truh

letter carrier (n)
un **facteur**
fak-tuhr
une **facteure**
fak-tuhr

lettuce (n)
une **laitue**
lay-tew

level (adj)
plat (m) **plate** (f)
pla/plat

library (n)
une **bibliothèque**
bee-blee-yo-tek

lid (n)
un **couvercle**
koo-vair-kluh

life (n)
la **vie**
vee

lifeboat (n)
un **bateau**
de sauvetage
ba-toh duh sohv-tazh

lifeguard (n)
un **surveillant**
de baignade
soor-vay-ah(n)
duh bayn-yad

life jacket (n)
un **gilet**
de sauvetage
zhee-lay duh sohv-tazh

light (not heavy)
(adj)
léger (m) **légère** (f)
lay-zhay/lay-zhehr

light (pale) (adj)
clair (m) **claire** (f)
klair

light (n)
une **lumière**
lewm-yair

lighthouse (n)
un **phare**
far

lightning (n)
un **éclair**
ay-klair

like (prep)
comme
kom

line (n)
une **ligne**
leen-ye

lineup (n)
une **queue**
kuh

lion (n)
un **lion**
lee-yo(n)

liquid (n)
un **liquide**
lee-keed

lizard
le lézard

list (n)
une liste
leest

little (adj)
petit (m) petite (f)
puh-tee/puh-teet

living room (n)
un salon
sal-o(n)

lizard (n)
un lézard
lay-zar

long (adj)
long (m) longue (f)
lo(n)/lon-guh

(a) lot (adj)
beaucoup
boh-koo

loud (adj)
bruyant (m)
brew-yah(n)
bruyante (f)
brew-yahnt

lovely (adj)
adorable
a-do-ra-bluh

low (adj)
bas (m) basse (f)
bah/bahss

lucky (adj)
chanceux (m)
shahn-suh
chanceuse (f)
shahn-suhz

luggage (n)
les bagages (m)
bag-azh

lunch (n)
le déjeuner
day-zhuh-nay

lunch box (n)
une boîte à lunch
bwat ah lunch

M

magnet
l'aimant

machine (n)
une machine
ma-sheen

magazine (n)
un magazine
ma-ga-zeen

magician (n)
un magicien
ma-zhee-sya(n)
une magicienne
ma-zhee-syen

magnet (n)
un aimant
eh-mah(n)

magnetic (adj)
magnétique
man-yet-eek

magnifying glass (n)
une loupe
loop

mail (n)
la poste
post

mailbox (n)
une boîte
aux lettres
bwat oh let-truh

mailman (n)
un facteur
fak-tuhr
une facteure
fak-tuhr

main (adj)
principal (m)
principale (f)
prahn-see-pal

makeup (n)
le maquillage
ma-kee-yazh

male (human) (n)
un homme
om

mammal (n)
un mammifère
ma-mee-fair

man (n)
un homme
om

map (n)
une carte
kart

marbles (toy) (n)
les billes (f)
bee-ye

market (n)
un marché
mar-shay

married (adj)
marié (m) mariée (f)
mar-yay

mask (n)
un masque
mask

mat (n)
un petit tapis
puh-tee ta-pee

match (sport) (n)
un match
match

matchbox (n)
une boîte
d'allumettes
bwat dal-lew-met

math (n)
les mathématiques (f)
ma-tay-ma-teek

maybe (adv)
peut-être
puht-eh-truh

me (pron)
me/m' (vowel)
muh/m

meal (n)
un repas
ruh-pah

meaning (n)
un sens
sahnss

measurement (n)
une mesure
muh-zewr

meat (n)
la viande
vyahnd

medication (n)
un médicament
may-dee-ka-mah(n)

melon
le melon

tail
la queue

A B C D E F G H I J K L M N O P Q R S T U V W X Y Z

A
B
C
D
E
F
G
H
I
J
K
L
(M)
N
O
P
Q
R
S
T
U
V
W
X
Y
Z

milkshake
le lait frappé

melon (n)
un melon
muh-lo(n)

menu (n)
la carte
kart

mess (n)
le désordre
day-zor-druh

message (n)
un message
mess-azh

microwave (n)
un micro-ondes
mee-kro-ond

middle (n)
le milieu
meel-yuh

midnight (n)
minuit
mee-nwee

milk (n)
le lait
lay

milkshake (n)
un lait frappé
lay frah-pay

million
million
meel-yo(n)

mineral (n)
un minéral
mee-nay-ral

minute (n)
une minute
mee-newt

mirror (n)
un miroir
meer-wahr

mistake (n)
une erreur
er-ruhr

mitten (n)
une mitaine
mee-tehn

mixture (n)
un mélange
may-lahnzh

modelling clay (n)
la pâte à modeler
paht ah mod-lay

mom (n)
maman (f)
mah-mah(n)

money (n)
l'argent (m)
lar-zhah(n)

monkey (n)
un singe
sanzh

monster (n)
un monstre
mon-struh

mitten
la mitaine

month (n)
un mois
mwa

moon (n)
la lune
lewn

more than
plus que
plews kuh

morning (n)
le matin
ma-ta(n)

mosque (n)
une mosquée
mos-kay

moth (n)
un papillon de nuit
pa-pee-yo(n) duh nwee

mother (n)
une mère
mair

motor (n)
un moteur
mo-tuhr

motorcycle (n)
une moto
moh-toh

mountain (n)
une montagne
mon-tan-ye

mountain bike (n)
un vélo
de montagne
vay-lo duh mon-tan-ye

mouse (animal) (n)
une souris
soo-ree

**mouse
(computer) (n)**
une souris
soo-ree

mouse pad (n)
un tapis de souris
ta-pee duh soo-ree

moustache (n)
une moustache
moo-stash

mouth (n)
une bouche
boosh

movie theatre (n)
un cinéma
see-nay-ma

MP3 player (n)
un lecteur MP3
lek-tuhr em-pay-trwa

mud (n)
la boue
boo

muddy (adj)
boueux (m)
boo-uh
boueuse (f)
boo-uhz

mug (n)
une tasse
tahss

museum (n)
un musée
mew-zay

mushroom (n)
un champignon
shahm-peen-yo(n)

music (n)
la musique
mew-zeek

musician (n)
un musicien
mew-zee-sya(n)
une musicienne
mew-zee-syen

my (adj)
mon (m) ma (f)
mo(n)/ma

mushroom
le champignon

N

necklace
le collier

nail (n)
un ongle
ong-luh

name (n)
un nom
no(m)

narrow (adj)
étroit (m) étroite (f)
ay-trwa/ay-trwat

nature (n)
la nature
nat-ewr

naughty (adj)
vilain (m)
vee-la(n)
vilaine (f)
veelehn

nest
le nid

---

near (prep)
près de
preh duh

nearly (adv)
presque
presk

neck (n)
un cou
koo

necklace (n)
un collier
kol-yay

needle (n)
une aiguille
ehg-wee-ye

neighbour (n)
un voisin
vwa-za(n)
une voisine
vwa-zeen

nephew (n)
un neveu
nuh-vuh

nest (n)
un nid
nee

net (n)
une épuisette
ay-pwee-zet

never (adv)
jamais
z ha-may

new (adj)
nouveau (m)
noo-voh
nouvelle (f)
noo-vel

news (n)
les nouvelles (f)
noo-vel

newspaper (n)
un journal
zhoor-nal

---

next (adj)
prochain (m)
prosh-a(n)
prochaine (f)
prosh-ehn

nice (adj)
sympathique
sam-pa-teek

niece (n)
une nièce
nyehs

night (n)
la nuit
nwee

nobody (pron)
personne
pair-son

noisy (adj)
bruyant (m)
brew-yah(n)
bruyante (f)
brew-yahnt

noodles (n)
les nouilles (f)
noo-ye

north (n)
le nord
nor

nose (n)
un nez
nay

note (n)
un billet
bee-yay

noodles
les nouilles

notebook (n)
un carnet
kar-nay

nothing (n/pron)
rien
rya(n)

now (adv)
maintenant
mehn-tuh-nah(n)

nowhere (adv)
nulle part
newl par

number (n)
un nombre
nom-bruh

nurse (n)
une infirmière
an-feerm-yair

felt-tip pen
le feutre

notebook
le carnet

A
B
C
D
E
F
G
H
I
J
K
L
M
(N)
O
P
Q
R
S
T
U
V
W
X
Y
Z

A B C D E F G H I J K L M N (O) P Q R S T U V W X Y Z

ocean
l'océan

oar (n)
une **rame**
ram

object (n)
un **objet**
ob-zhay

ocean (n)
un **océan**
o-say-ah(n)

office (n)
un **bureau**
bew-roh

often (adv)
souvent
soo-vah(n)

onion
l'oignon

oil (n)
l'**huile** (f)
lweel

old (adj)
vieux (m) vieille (f)
vyuh/vyay

old person (n)
une **personne âgée**
pair-son ah-zhay

Olympic Games (n)
les **Jeux olympiques** (m)
zhuz o-leem-peek

on top of (prep)
sur
sewr

onion (n)
un **oignon**
ohn-yo(n)

only (adv)
seulement
suhl-mah(n)

open (adj)
ouvert (m)
oo-vair
ouverte (f)
oo-vairt

opening hours (n)
les **heures d'ouverture** (f)
uhr doo-vair-tewr

orange
l'orange

orange juice
le jus d'orange

operation (n)
une **opération**
o-pair-a-syo(n)

opposite (n)
un **contraire**
kon-trair

opposite (prep)
en **face de**
ah(n) fass duh

or (conj)
ou
oo

orange (colour) (adj)
orange
or-ahnzh

orange (fruit) (n)
une **orange**
or-ahnzh

orange juice (n)
un **jus d'orange**
zhew dor-ahnzh

orchestra (n)
un **orchestre**
or-ke-struh

other (adj)
autre
oh-truh

ouch!
aïe !
eye-ye

our (adj)
notre (m/f)
no-truh

out of (prep)
hors de
or duh

outside (adv)
dehors
duh-or

oval (n)
un **ovale**
o-val

oven (n)
un **four**
foor

oven mitt (n)
un **gant de cuisine**
gah(n) duh kwee-zeen

over there (adv)
là-bas
la-bah

owl (n)
un **hibou**
ee-boo

own (adj)
propre
pro-pruh

owl
le hibou

P

paint can
le pot de peinture

page (n)
une **page**
pazh

paint (n)
la **peinture**
pan-tewr

paintbrush (n)
un **pinceau**
pan-soh

paint can (n)
un **pot de peinture**
poh duh pan-tewr

pair (n)
une **paire**
pair

palm tree (n)
un **palmier**
palm-yay

pancake (n)
une **crêpe**
krehp

panda (n)
un **panda**
pahn-da

pants (n)
un **pantalon**
pahn-ta-lo(n)

paper (n)
le **papier**
pap-yay

paper clip (n)
un **trombone**
trom-bon

paper towel (n)
un **essuie-tout**
es-swee too

parade (n)
un **défilé**
day-fee-lay

parent (n)
un **parent**
par-ah(n)

park (n)
un **parc**
park

parrot (n)
un **perroquet**
pair-o-kay

part (n)
une **partie**
par-tee

party (n)
une **fête**
feht

passenger (n)
un **passager**
pah-sa-zhay
une **passagère**
pah-sa-zhair

passport (n)
un **passeport**
pah-spor

past (history) (n)
le **passé**
pah-say

past (prep)
après
ap-reh

pasta (n)
les **pâtes** (f)
paht

path (n)
un **chemin**
shuh-ma(n)

patient (adj)
patient (m)
pa-sya(n)
patiente (f)
pa-syant

patient (n)
un **patient**
pa-sya(n)
une **patiente**
pa-syant

pattern (n)
un **motif**
mo-teef

paw (n)
une **patte**
pat

pay (n)
un **salaire**
sa-lair

pea (n)
un **pois**
pwa

peace (n)
la **paix**
pay

peaceful (adj)
tranquille
trahn-keel

pear
la poire

peanut (n)
une **cacahuète**
ka-ka-weht

pear (n)
une **poire**
pwahr

pebble (n)
un **galet**
ga-lay

pedal (n)
une **pédale**
pay-dal

pelican (n)
un **pélican**
pay-lee-kah(n)

pen (n)
un **stylo**
stee-loh

pelican
le pélican

beak
le bec

wing
l'aile

A B C D E F G H I J K L M N O P Q R S T U V W X Y Z

79

A B C D E F G H I J K L M N O P Q R S T U V W X Y Z

pencil (n)
un **crayon à mine**
kray-yo(n) ah meen

pencil case (n)
une **trousse**
trooss

penguin (n)
un **pingouin**
pa(n)-gwa(n)

pentagon (n)
un **pentagone**
pahn-ta-gon

people (n)
les **gens** (pl)
zhah(n)

pepper (n)
le **poivre**
pwa-vruh

perfect (adj)
parfait (m)
par-fay
parfaite (f)
par-feht

perhaps (adv)
peut-être
puh-teh-truh

person (n)
une **personne**
pair-son

pet (n)
un **animal familier**
an-ee-mal fa-meel-yay

phone (n)
un **téléphone**
tay-lay-fon

photo (n)
une **photo**
fo-toh

piano (n)
un **piano**
piano

picnic (n)
un **pique-nique**
peek-neek

picture (n)
une **image**
ee-mazh

piece (n)
un **morceau**
mor-soh

piano
le piano

pine cone
la pomme de pin

pig (n)
un **cochon**
ko-sho(n)

pillow (n)
un **oreiller**
o-ray-yay

pilot (n)
un **pilote**
pee-lot

pineapple (n)
un **ananas**
an-an-ass

pine cone (n)
une **pomme de pin**
pom duh pa(n)

pine tree (n)
un **pin**
pa(n)

pink (adj)
rose
rohz

pizza (n)
une **pizza**
peed-za

place (n)
un **endroit**
ahn-drwa

plane (n)
un **avion**
av-yo(n)

planet (n)
une **planète**
plan-eht

plant (n)
une **plante**
plahnt

plastic (adj)
en **plastique**
ah(n) plas-teek

plastic bag (n)
un **sac en plastique**
sak ah(n) plas-teek

plate (n)
une **assiette**
a-syet

play (n)
une **pièce de théâtre**
pyehs duh tay-a-truh

player (n)
un **joueur**
zhoo-uhr
une **joueuse**
zhoo-uhz

playground (n)
un **terrain de jeu**
tair-ra(n) duh zhuh

pine tree
le pin

playtime (n)
une **récréation**
ray-kray-a-syo(n)

please (adv)
s'il te plaît
seel tuh pleh

plug (for bath) (n)
un **bouchon**
boo-sho(n)

plug (electric) (n)
une **prise électrique**
preez ay-lek-treek

pocket (n)
une **poche**
posh

pocket money (n)
l'argent de poche (m)
lar-zhah(n) duh posh

point (n)
un **point**
pwa(n)

polar bear (n)
un **ours polaire**
oorss po-lair

pole (post) (n)
un **poteau**
po-toh

police (n)
la **police**
po-leess

police car (n)
une **voiture de police**
vwa-tewr duh po-leess

police helicopter (n)
un **hélicoptère de police**
ay-lee-kop-tair duh po-leess

police officer (n)
un **policier**
po-lee-syay
une **policière**
po-lee-see-yair

polite (adj)
poli (m) polie (f)
po-lee

pond (n)
un **étang**
ay-tah(n)

poor (adj)
pauvre
poh-vruh

popular (adj)
populaire
po-pew-lair

possible (adj)
possible
po-see-bluh

postal code (n)
un **code postal**
kohd pos-tal

postcard (n)
une **carte postale**
kart pos-tal

poster (n)
une **affiche**
af-feesh

postman (n)
un **facteur**
fak-tuhr
une **facteure**
fak-tuhr

post office (n)
un **bureau de poste**
bew-roh duh post

potato (n)
une **pomme de terre**
pom duh tair

pouch (n)
une **pochette**
po-shet

powder (n)
la **poudre**
poo-druh

present (n)
un **cadeau**
ka-doh

puppy
le chiot

president (n)
un **président (m)**
pray-zee-dah(n)
une **presidente (f)**
pray-zee-dah(n)t

pretty (adj)
joli (m) jolie (f)
zho-lee

price (n)
un **prix**
pree

prince (n)
un **prince**
pranss

princess (n)
une **princesse**
pran-sess

prize (n)
un **prix**
pree

probably (adv)
probablement
pro-bab-luh-mah(n)

problem (n)
un **problème**
prob-lehm

program (TV) (n)
une **émission**
ay-mee-syo(n)

project (n)
un **projet**
pro-zhay

pumpkin (n)
une **citrouille**
see-troo-ye

pupil (n)
un/une **élève**
ay-lehv

puppet (n)
une **marionnette**
mar-yon-net

puppy (n)
un **chiot**
shyoh

purple (adj)
violet (m) violette (f)
vyo-lay/vyo-let

purse (n)
un **sac à main**
sak ah ma(n)

puzzle (n)
un **casse-tête**
kahs-teht

pyjamas (n)
un **pyjama**
pee-zha-ma

pouch
la pochette

A
B
C
D
E
F
G
H
I
J
K
L
M
N
O
(P)
Q
R
S
T
U
V
W
X
Y
Z

A
B
C
D
E
F
G
H
I
J
K
L
M
N
O
P
Q
R
S
T
U
V
W
X
Y
Z

Q R

quarter (n)
un **quart**
kar

queen (n)
une **reine**
rehn

question (n)
une **question**
kest-yo(n)

quickly (adv)
vite
veet

quiet (adj)
silencieux (m)
see-lahn-syuh
silencieuse (f)
see-lahn-syuhz

quietly (adv)
tranquillement
trahn-keel-mah(n)

quiz (n)
un **quiz**
kweez

queen
la reine

rabbit (n)
un **lapin**
lap-a(n)

race (n)
une **course**
koorss

race car (n)
une **voiture**
de course
vwa-tewr duh koorss

racquet (n)
une **raquette**
rak-et

radio (n)
une **radio**
rad-yo

railway station (n)
une **gare**
gar

rain (n)
la **pluie**
plwee

rainbow (n)
un **arc-en-ciel**
ark-ah(n)-syel

raincoat (n)
un **imperméable**
am-pair-may-a-bluh

race car
la voiture
de course

rainforest (n)
la **forêt tropicale**
for-eh tro-pee-kal

rake (n)
un **râteau**
rah-toh

raspberry (n)
une **framboise**
frahm-bwaz

rat (n)
un **rat**
ra

reading (n)
la **lecture**
lek-tewr

ready (adj)
prêt (m)
preh
prête (f)
preht

real (adj)
réel (m) réelle (f)
ray-el

really (adv)
vraiment
vray-mah(n)

receipt (n)
un **reçu**
ruh-sew

recipe (n)
une **recette**
ruh-set

rectangle (n)
un **rectangle**
rek-tahn-gluh

red (adj)
rouge
roozh

referee (n)
un **arbitre**
ar-bee-truh

religion (n)
la **religion**
ruh-lee-zhyo(n)

remote control (n)
une **télécommande**
tay-lay-kom-mahnd

report
(for school) (n)
un **exposé**
ek-spoh-zay

rescue (n)
les **secours (m)**
suh-koor

restaurant (n)
un **restaurant**
res-tor-ah(n)

reward (n)
une **récompense**
ray-kom-pah(n)s

rhinoceros (n)
un **rhinocéros**
ree-no-say-ros

ribbon (n)
un **ruban**
rew-bah(n)

rice (n)
le **riz**
ree

rich (adj)
riche
reesh

S

right (not left) (adj)
droit (m) droite (f)
drwa/drwat

right (correct) (adj)
exact (m) exacte (f)
eg-zakt

ring (n)
une bague
bag

ripe (adj)
mûr (m) mûre (f)
mewr

river (n)
une rivière
reev-yehr

road (n)
une route
root

robot (n)
un robot
ro-boh

rock (n)
une roche
rosh

rocket (n)
une fusée
few-zay

roll (bread) (n)
un petit pain
puh-tee pa(n)

roof (n)
un toit
twa

room (n)
une pièce
pyehs

root (n)
une racine
ra-seen

rope (n)
une corde
cord

rose (n)
une rose
rohz

rough (adj)
rugueux (m)
rew-ghuh
rugueuse (f)
rew-ghuhz

round (adj)
rond (m)
ro(n)
ronde (f)
rond

route (n)
un trajet
tra-zhay

rowboat (n)
une chaloupe
sha-loop

rubber band (n)
un élastique
ay-la-steek

rug (n)
un tapis
ta-pee

rugby (n)
le rugby
rewg-bee

ruler (measure) (n)
une règle
reh-gluh

running (n)
la course à pied
koorss ah pyay

running shoes (n)
les espadrilles
ehs-pa-dree-ye

runway (n)
une piste
peest

saddle
la selle

sack (n)
un sac
sak

sad (adj)
triste
treest

saddle (n)
une selle
sel

safe (adj)
en sécurité
ah(n) say-kew-ree-tay

sail (n)
une voile
vwal

sailboat (n)
un bateau à voiles
ba-toh ah vwal

sailor (n)
un marin
mar-a(n)

salad (n)
une salade
sal-ad

sales person (n)
un vendeur
vahn-duhr
une vendeuse
vahn-duhz

salt (n)
le sel
sel

same (adj)
même
mehm

sand (n)
le sable
sah-bluh

sandal (n)
une sandale
sahn-dal

sandcastle (n)
un château de sable
sha-toh duh sah-bluh

sandwich (n)
un sandwich
sahnd-weetsh

saucepan (n)
une casserole
kass-rol

scarf (n)
un foulard
foo-lahr

school (n)
l'école (f)
lay-kol

school bag (n)
un sac d'école
sak day-kol

scarf
le foulard

A B C D E F G H I J K L M N O P Q ⓇⓈ T U V W X Y Z

A
B
C
D
E
F
G
H
I
J
K
L
M
N
O
P
Q
R
(S)
T
U
V
W
X
Y
Z

scissors
les ciseaux

school uniform (n)
un **uniforme**
scolaire
ew-nee-form sko-lair

science (n)
les **sciences**
see-yahnss

scientist (n)
un/une
scientifique
see-yahn-tee-feek

scissors (n)
les **ciseaux**
see-zoh

screen (n)
un **écran**
ay-krah(n)

sea (n)
la **mer**
mair

seagull (n)
une **mouette**
moo-wet

seal (n)
un **phoque**
fok

sea lion (n)
un **lion de mer**
lee-yo(n) duh mair

seaside (n)
le **bord de la mer**
bor duh la mair

season (n)
une **saison**
seh-zo(n)

seaweed (n)
une **algue**
al-guh

second (2nd) (adj)
deuxième
duhz-yehm

second (time) (n)
une **seconde**
suh-go(n)

seed (n)
une **graine**
grehn

semicircle (n)
un **demi-cercle**
duh-mee sair-kluh

shallow (adj)
peu profond (m)
puh pro-fo(n)
peu profonde (f)
puh pro-fond

shampoo (n)
un **shampooing**
shahm-pwa(n)

shape (n)
une **forme**
form

shark (n)
un **requin**
ruh-ka(n)

sharp (adj)
aigu (m) aiguë (f)
ehg-ew

she (pron)
elle
el

sheep (n)
un **mouton**
moo-to(n)

sheepdog (n)
un **chien de berger**
shya(n) duh bair-zhay

sheet (for bed) (n)
un **drap**
dra

shelf (n)
une **étagère**
ay-ta-zhehr

shell (n)
un **coquillage**
ko-kee-yazh

shiny (adj)
brillant (m)
bree-yah(n)
brillante (f)
bree-yahnt

ship (n)
un **navire**
na-veer

shirt (n)
une **chemise**
shuh-meez

shoe (n)
une **chaussure**
shoh-soor

shopper (n)
un **acheteur**
ash-tuhr
une **acheteuse**
ash-tuhz

wool
la laine

sheep
le mouton

shopping (n)
les **courses (f)**
koorss

shopping bag (n)
un **sac**
sak

shopping list (n)
une **liste**
de courses
leest duh koorss

short (adj)
court (m) courte (f)
koor/koort

shorts (n)
un **short**
short

shoulder (n)
une **épaule**
ay-pohl

show (n)
un **spectacle**
spek-ta-kluh

shower (n)
une **douche**
doosh

shy (adj)
timide
tee-meed

sick (adj)
malade
ma-lad

sidewalk (n)
un **trottoir**
trot-wahr

sign (n)
un **panneau de**
signalisation
pan-noh duh
seen-ya-lee-za-syo(n)

silver (n)
l'**argent (m)**
lar-zhah(n)

simple (adj)
simple
sam-pluh

helmet
le casque

t-shirt
le tee-shirt

shorts
le short

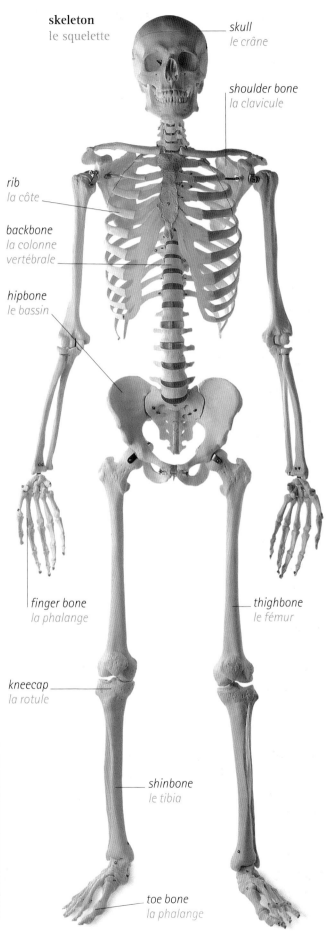

skeleton
le squelette

skull
le crâne

shoulder bone
la clavicule

rib
la côte

backbone
*la colonne
vertébrale*

hipbone
le bassin

finger bone
la phalange

thighbone
le fémur

kneecap
la rotule

shinbone
le tibia

toe bone
la phalange

singing (n)
le **chant**
shah(n)

sink (bathroom) (n)
un **lavabo**
la-va-boh

sink (kitchen) (n)
un **évier**
ayv-yay

sister (n)
une **sœur**
suhr

size (n)
la **taille**
tah-ye

skateboard (n)
une **planche
à roulettes**
plahnsh a roo-leht

skeleton (n)
un **squelette**
skuh-let

skiing (n)
le **ski**
skee

skin (n)
la **peau**
poh

skipping rope (n)
une **corde à sauter**
kord ah soh-tay

skirt (n)
une **jupe**
zhewp

sky (n)
le **ciel**
syel

skyscraper (n)
un **gratte-ciel**
grat-syel

sleeping bag (n)
un **sac de couchage**
sak duh koosh-azh

sleeve (n)
une **manche**
mahnsh

sleigh (n)
un **traîneau**
treh-noh

slipper (n)
une **pantoufle**
pahn-too-fluh

slow (adj)
lent (m) lente (f)
lah(n)/lahnt

A
B
C
D
E
F
G
H
I
J
K
L
M
N
O
P
Q
R
Ⓢ
T
U
V
W
X
Y
Z

snake
le serpent

tail
la queue

head
la tête

slowly (adv)
lentement
lahn-tuh-mah(n)

small (adj)
petit (m) petite (f)
puh-tee/puh-teet

smart (adj)
élégant (m)
ay-lay-gahhn)
élégante (f)
ay-lay-gahnt

smell (n)
une odeur
o-duhr

smoke (n)
la fumée
few-may

smooth (adj)
lisse
leess

snail (n)
un escargot
es-kar-goh

snake (n)
un serpent
sair-pah(n)

snow (n)
la neige
nehzh

snail
l'escargot

snowball (n)
une boule de neige
bool duh nehzh

snowboard (n)
une planche
à neige
plahnsh a nehzh

snowflake (n)
un flocon de neige
flo-ko(n) duh nehzh

snowman (n)
un bonhomme
de neige
bon-om duh nehzh

soap (n)
le savon
sa-vo(n)

soccer (n)
le soccer
sok-uhr

soccer ball (n)
un ballon
de soccer
ba-lo(n) duh sok-uhr

sock (n)
un bas
bah

sofa (n)
un canapé
ka-na-pay

soft (adj)
mou (m) molle (f)
moo/mo-luh

soil (n)
la terre
tair

solid (n)
un solide
sol-eed

some (adj)
quelques
kel-kuh

someone (pron)
quelqu'un
kel-ka(n)

something (pron)
quelque chose
kel-kuh shohz

sometimes (adv)
quelquefois
kel-kuh fwa

son (n)
un fils
feess

soon (adv)
bientôt
byan-toh

south (n)
le sud
sewd

space (n)
l'espace (m)
less-pass

space rocket (n)
une fusée
few-zay

spade (n)
une pelle
pel

spaghetti (n)
les spaghettis (m)
spa-get-ee

special (adj)
particulier (m)
par-tee-kewl-yay
particulière (f)
par-tee-kewl-yair

speech (n)
un discours
dee-skoor

spider (n)
une araignée
ar-ehn-yay

sponge (n)
une éponge
ay-ponzh

spoon (n)
une cuillère
kwee-yehr

sport (n)
un sport
spor

spring (season) (n)
le printemps
pran-tah(m)

square (n)
un carré
kar-ray

squirrel (n)
un écureuil
ay-kew-ruh-ye

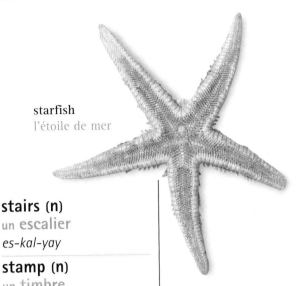

starfish
l'étoile de mer

stairs (n)
un **escalier**
es-kal-yay

stamp (n)
un **timbre**
tam-bruh

star (n)
une **étoile**
ay-twal

starfish (n)
une **étoile de mer**
ay-twal duh mair

station (n)
une **gare**
gar

steam (n)
la **buée**
bway

steep (adj)
raide
rehd

stem (n)
une **tige**
teezh

step (n)
un **pas**
pa

stepfather (n)
un **beau-père**
boh-pair

stepmother (n)
une **belle-mère**
bel-mair

stick (n)
un **bâton**
bah-to(n)

sticker (n)
un **autocollant**
oh-to-ko-lah(n)

sticky (adj)
collant (m)
ko-lah(n)
collante (f)
ko-lahnt

still (adj)
immobile
im-mob-eel

stocking (n)
un **bas**
bah

stomach (n)
un **estomac**
es-to-ma

stone (n)
une **pierre**
pyair

store (n)
un **magasin**
ma-ga-za(n)

storey (n)
un **étage**
ay-tazh

stormy (adj)
orageux (m)
or-azh-uh
orageuse (f)
or-azh-uhz

story (n)
une **histoire**
eest-wahr

stove (n)
une **cuisinière**
kwee-zeen-yair

straight (adj)
droit (m) **droite** (f)
drwa/drwat

strange (adj)
étrange
ay-trahnzh

straw (n)
la **paille**
pah-ye

strawberry (n)
une **fraise**
frehz

street (n)
une **rue**
rew

street light (n)
un **réverbère**
ray-vair-bair

strict (adj)
sévère
say-vehr

string (n)
une **ficelle**
fee-sel

stripes (n)
les **rayures**
ray-ewr

stroller (n)
une **poussette**
poo-set

strawberry
la fraise

strong (adj)
fort (m) **forte** (f)
for/fort

student (n)
un/une **élève**
ay-lehv

stupid (adj)
stupide
stoo-peed

subject (n)
un **sujet**
sew-zhay

submarine (n)
un **sous-marin**
soo-ma-ra(n)

subway (n)
un **métro**
may-troh

suddenly (adv)
tout à coup
toot ah koo

sugar (n)
le **sucre**
sew-kruh

suit (n)
un **costume**
kos-tewm

suitcase (n)
une **valise**
val-eez

summer (n)
l'**été** (m)
lay-tay

sunflower
le tournesol

A
B
C
D
E
F
G
H
I
J
K
L
M
N
O
P
Q
R
(S)
T
U
V
W
X
Y
Z

A
B
C
D
E
F
G
H
I
J
K
L
M
N
O
P
Q
R
Ⓢ
Ⓣ
U
V
W
X
Y
Z

sun (n)
le soleil
so-laye

sunflower (n)
un tournesol
toor-nuh-sol

sunglasses (n)
les lunettes
de soleil (f)
lew-net duh so-laye

sunhat (n)
un chapeau
de soleil
sha-poh duh so-laye

sunny (adj)
ensoleillé (m)
ensoleillée (f)
ahn-so-lay-yay

sunset (n)
un coucher de soleil
koo-shay duh so-laye

suntan lotion (n)
la crème solaire
krehm so-lair

supermarket (n)
un supermarché
soo-pair-mar-shay

sure (adj)
sûr (m) sûre (f)
sewr

surface (n)
une surface
soor-fass

sunglasses
les lunettes de soleil

surfboard (n)
une planche de surf
plahnsh duh surf

surfing (n)
le surf
surf

surgery (n)
une chirurgie
shee-ruhr-zhee

surprise (n)
une surprise
soor-preez

surprising (adj)
étonnant (m)
ay-ton-nah(n)
étonnante (f)
ay-ton-nahnt

swan (n)
un cygne
seen-ye

sweater (n)
un chandail
shahn-da-ye

swim goggles (n)
les lunettes de
natation (f)
lew-net duh na-ta-syo(n)

swimming (n)
la natation
na-ta-syo(n)

swimming pool (n)
une piscine
pee-seen

swing (n)
une balançoire
ba-lahn-swahr

tadpole
le têtard

table (n)
une table
tab-luh

table tennis (n)
le ping-pong
ping-pong

tadpole (n)
un têtard
teh-tar

tail (n)
une queue
kuh

tall (adj)
grand (m)
grah(n)
grande (f)
grahnd

tap (faucet) (n)
un robinet
ro-bee-nay

tape measure (n)
un mètre-ruban
meh-truh-rew-bah(n)

taxi (n)
un taxi
tak-see

tape measure
le mètre-ruban

tea (n)
le thé
tay

teacher (n)
un maître
meh-truh
une maîtresse
meh-tress

team (n)
une équipe
ay-keep

teddy bear (n)
un ours en peluche
oorss ah(n) puh-lewsh

telescope (n)
un télescope
tay-leh-skop

television (n)
la télévision
tay-lay-vee-zyo(n)

tennis (n)
le tennis
ten-neess

tent (n)
une tente
tahnt

term (n)
un mot
moh

terrible (adj)
terrible
tair-ee-bluh

test (n)
un examen
eg-za-ma(n)

text message (n)
un texto
teks-toh

that one (pron)
celui-là
suhl-wee-la

the (article)
le (m) la (f) l'(vowel)
luh/la/l

their (adj)
leur (m/f)
luhr

then (conj)
alors
al-or

there (adv)
là
la

thermometer (n)
un thermomètre
tair-mo-meh-truh

they (pron)
ils (m) elles (f)
eel/el

thick (adj)
épais (m) épaisse (f)
ay-pay/ay-pehss

thin (adj)
fin (m) fine (f)
fa(n)/feen

thing (n)
une chose
shohz

third (adj)
troisième
trwaz-yehm

thirsty (adj)
assoiffé (m)
assoiffée (f)
a-swa-fay

this one (pron)
celui-ci
suhl-wee-see

thousand
mille
meel

through (prep)
à travers
ah tra-vair

thumb (n)
un pouce
pooss

thumb tack (n)
une punaise
pew-nehz

thunderstorm (n)
un orage
or-azh

ticket (n)
un billet
bee-yay

tide (n)
la marée
ma-ray

toad
le crapaud

tongue
la langue

tie (n)
une cravate
kra-vat

tiger (n)
un tigre
tee-gruh

tight (adj)
serré (m) serrée (f)
sair-ray

tights
les collants (m)
ko-lah(n)

time (n)
l'heure (f)
luhr

timetable (n)
un horaire
or-air

tiny (adj)
minuscule
mee-new-skewl

tire (n)
un pneu
p-nuh

tired (adj)
fatigué (m)
fatiguée (f)
fa-tee-gay

tissues (n)
les papiers-
mouchoirs
pap-yay moosh-wahr

toad (n)
un crapaud
kra-poh

toaster (n)
un grille-pain
gree-ye-pa(n)

today (adv)
aujourd'hui
oh-zhoor-dwee

toe (n)
un orteil
or-teye

together (adv)
ensemble
ahn-sahm-bluh

toilet (n)
les toilettes
twa-let

toilet paper (n)
le papier hygiénique
pap-yay ee-zhen-eek

tomato (n)
une tomate
tom-at

whiskers
les moustaches

stripes
les rayures

tail
la queue

tiger
le tigre

A
B
C
D
E
F
G
H
I
J
K
L
M
N
O
P
Q
R
S
(T)
U
V
W
X
Y
Z

A
B
C
D
E
F
G
H
I
J
K
L
M
N
O
P
Q
R
S
(T)
U
V
W
X
Y
Z

toothbrush
la brosse à dents

tomorrow (adv)
demain
duh-ma(n)

tongue (n)
une langue
lahn-guh

tonight (adv)
cette nuit
set nwee

too (adv)
aussi
oh-see

tool (n)
un outil
oo-tee

tooth (n)
une dent
dah(n)

toothbrush (n)
une brosse à dents
bros ah dah(n)

toothpaste (n)
le dentifrice
dahn-tee-freess

top (n)
le haut
oh

tortoise
la tortue

toque (n)
une tuque
tew-kuh

tornado (n)
une tornade
tor-nad

tortoise (n)
une tortue
tor-tew

toucan (n)
un toucan
too-kah(n)

tough (adj)
dur (m) dure (f)
dewr

tourist (n)
un/une touriste
too-reest

toward (prep)
vers
vair

towel (n)
une serviette
sair-vee-et

town (n)
une ville
veel

toy (n)
un jouet
zhoo-way

toy blocks (n)
les cubes (m)
kewb

toy box (n)
un coffre à jouets
kof-fruh ah zhoo-way

tractor (n)
un tracteur
trak-tuhr

traffic (n)
la circulation
seer-kew-lah-syo(n)

traffic lights
les feux de signalisation

traffic lights (n)
les feux de
signalisation (m)
fuh duh
seen-ya-lee-za-syo(n)

train (n)
un train
tra(n)

train set (toy) (n)
un train
tra(n)

transport (n)
le transport
trahn-spor

tray (n)
un plateau
pla-toh

tree (n)
un arbre
ar-bruh

triangle (n)
un triangle
tree-yahn-gluh

trip (n)
un voyage
vwa-yazh

tropical (adj)
tropical (m)
tropicale (f)
tro-pee-kal

trouble (n)
un ennui
ahn-wee

trowel (n)
un transplantoir
trahns-plahnt-wahr

truck (n)
un camion
kam-yo(n)

true (adj)
vrai (m) vraie (f)
vray

trunk (animal) (n)
une trompe
tromp

trunk (tree) (n)
un tronc
tro(n)

trunk
la trompe

90

turkey
le dindon

T-shirt (n)
un tee-shirt
tee-shirt

tube (n)
un tube
tewb

tummy (n)
un ventre
vahn-truh

tunnel (n)
un tunnel
tew-nel

turkey (n)
un dindon
dan-do(n)

turn (bend) (n)
un tournant
toor-nah(n)

turtle (n)
une tortue de mer
tor-tew duh mair

twice (adv)
deux fois
duh fwa

twin (n)
un jumeau
zhew-moh
une jumelle
zhew-mel

U

ugly (adj)
laid (m) laide (f)
lay/lehd

umbrella (rain) (n)
un parapluie
pa-ra-plwee

umbrella (sun) (n)
un parasol
pa-ra-sol

uncle (n)
un oncle
onk-luh

under (prep)
sous
soo

underwear (n)
les sous-vêtements (m)
soo-veht-mah(n)

unfair (adj)
injuste
an-zhewst

uniform (n)
un uniforme
ew-nee-form

umbrella
le parapluie

uniform
l'uniforme

universe (n)
un univers
ew-nee-vair

until (prep)
jusqu'à
zhew-ska

unusual (adj)
inhabituel (m)
inhabituelle (f)
een-ab-ee-tew-el

upside down (adv)
à l'envers
ah lahn-vair

upstairs (adv)
en haut
ah(n) oh

useful (adj)
utile
ew-teel

usually (adv)
d'habitude
da-bee-tewd

vacation (n)
les vacances (f)
vak-ahnss

van (n)
une camionnette
kam-yon-net

vegetable (n)
un légume
lay-gewm

vegetarian (n)
un végétarien
vay-zhay-ta-rya(n)
une végétarienne
vay-zhay-ta-ryen

verb (n)
un verbe
vairb

very (adv)
très
treh

vet (n)
un/une vétérinaire
vay-tair-ee-nair

video game (n)
un jeu vidéo
zhuh vee-day-oh

violin (n)
un violon
vyo-lo(n)

voice (n)
une voix
vwa

V

violin
le violon

A
B
C
D
E
F
G
H
I
J
K
L
M
N
O
P
Q
R
S
(T)
(U)
(V)
W
X
Y
Z

A B C D E F G H I J K L M N O P Q R S T U V **(W)** X Y Z

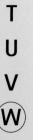

waist (n)
la **taille**
tah-ye

waiter (n)
un **serveur**
sair-vuh

waitress (n)
une **serveuse**
sair-vuhz

walk (n)
une **promenade**
pro-muh-nad

wall (n)
un **mur**
mewr

wallet (n)
un **porte-monnaie**
port-mo-nay

war (n)
une **guerre**
gair

wardrobe (n)
une **armoire**
arm-wahr

warm (adj)
chaud (m)
chaude (f)
shoh/shohd

warning (n)
un **avertissement**
av-air-tee-smah(n)

washing machine (n)
une **machine à laver**
ma-sheen ah la-vay

watering can
l'arrosoir

wasp (n)
une **guêpe**
gehp

watch (n)
une **montre**
mon-truh

water (n)
l'**eau (f)**
loh

watering can (n)
un **arrosoir**
ar-rohz-wahr

water lily (n)
un **nénuphar**
nay-new-far

watermelon (n)
un **melon d'eau**
muh-lo(n) doh

waterslide (n)
une **glissade d'eau**
glee-sad doh

wave (n)
une **vague**
vag

wave
la vague

wavy (adj)
ondulé
oh(n)-du-lay

we (pron)
nous
noo

weak (adj)
faible
fay-bluh

weather (n)
le **temps**
tah(n)

website (n)
un **site web**
seet web

weed (n)
une **mauvaise herbe**
moh-vayz airb

week (n)
une **semaine**
suh-mehn

weekend (n)
une **fin de semaine**
fa(n) duh suh-mehn

welcome (adj)
bienvenu (m)
bienvenue (f)
byan-vuh-new

well (adj)
bien
bya(n)

west (n)
l'**ouest (m)**
lwest

wet (adj)
mouillé (m)
mouillée (f)
moo-yay

whale (n)
une **baleine**
ba-len

wheat (n)
le **blé**
blay

wheel (n)
une **roue**
roo

wheelbarrow (n)
une **brouette**
broo-et

wheelchair (n)
un **fauteuil roulant**
foh-tuh-ye roo-lah(n)

when (adv)
quand
kah(n)

where (adv)
où
oo

while (conj)
pendant que
pahn-dah(n) kuh

whisker (n)
une **moustache**
moo-stash

whistle (n)
un **sifflement**
see-fluh-mah(n)

white (adj)
blanc (m)
blanche (f)
blah(n)/blahnsh

who (pron)
qui
kee

wing
l'aile

why (adv)
pourquoi
poor-kwa

wide (adj)
large
larzh

wife (n)
une épouse
ay-pooz

wind (n)
le vent
vah(n)

window (n)
une fenêtre
fuh-neh-truh

windy (adj)
venteux
vahn-tuh

wing (n)
une aile
ehl

winner (n)
un gagnant
gan-yah(n)
une gagnante
gan-yahnt

winter (n)
l'hiver (m)
lee-vair

wish (n)
un souhait
soo-way

with (prep)
avec
av-ek

without (prep)
sans
sah(n)

wolf (n)
un loup
loo

woman (n)
une femme
fam

wood (n)
le bois
bwa

wooden (adj)
en bois
ah(n) bwa

wool (n)
la laine
lehn

word (n)
un mot
moh

world (n)
un monde
mond

worm (n)
un ver
vair

worst (adj)
pire
peer

writing (act of) (n)
l'écriture (f)
lay-kree-tewr

yacht
le yacht

yacht (n)
un yacht
yoht

year (n)
une année
un an (for numbers)
an-nay/ah(n)

yellow (adj)
jaune
zhohn

yesterday (adv)
hier
yair

yogourt (n)
un yogourt
yoh-goor

you (pron)
tu/vous
tew/voo

young (adj)
jeune
zhuhn

your (adj)
votre
vo-truh

zebra
le zèbre

zebra (n)
un zèbre
zeh-bruh

zipper (n)
une fermeture éclair
fair-muh-tewr ay-klair

zone (n)
une zone
zohn

zoo (n)
un zoo
zoh

zipper
la fermeture éclair

A
B
C
D
E
F
G
H
I
J
K
L
M
N
O
P
Q
R
S
T
U
V
W
X
Y
Z

ABCDEFGHIJKLMNOPQRSTUVWXYZ

French A–Z

In this section, French words are in alphabetical order. They are followed by the English translation and a few letters to show what type of word it is—a noun (n) or adjective (adj), for example. Look at p.56 to see a list of the different types of words.

Nouns in French are either masculine or feminine. We have used (m) and (f) to tell you which they are.

Sometimes a word in French might mean more than one thing in English, so there might be two translations underneath.

Most of the nouns (naming words) here are singular (only one of the object). To make a noun plural (for more than one thing) you usually just add an "s"—the same as in English. In French though, the other words in the sentence change too—*le* and *la* become *les*. The adjectives also change, usually getting an extra "s" at the end.

à l'arrière (adv)
back (opposite of front)

à l'envers (adv)
upside down

à l'intérieur de (prep)
inside

à la mode (adv)
fashionable

à travers (prep)
through

abeille (n) (f)
bee

absent/absente (adj)
away

accident (n) (m)
accident

acheteur/acheteuse (n) (m/f)
shopper

activité (n) (f)
activity

adorable (adj)
lovely

adresse (n) (f)
address

adresse électronique (n) (f)
email address

adulte (n) (m/f)
adult

aéroport (n) (m)
airport

affaires (n) (f)
business

affamé/affamée (adj)
hungry

affiche (n) (f)
poster

âge (n) (m)
age

agneau (n) (m)
lamb

aide (n) (f)
help

aïe !
ouch!

aigle (n) (m)
eagle

aigu/aiguë (adj)
sharp

aiguille (n) (f)
needle

aile (n) (f)
wing

aimant (n) (m)
magnet

air (n) (m)
air

algue (n) (f)
seaweed

alligator (n) (m)
alligator

alors (conj)
then

alphabet (n) (m)
alphabet

ambulance (n) (f)
ambulance

ami/amie (n) (m/f)
friend

amical/amicale (adj)
friendly

ampoule (n) (f)
bulb (light)

amusant/amusante (adj)
fun

amusement (n) (m)
fun

ananas (n) (m)
pineapple

ancre (n) (f)
anchor

anglais (n) (m)
English

animal (n) (m)
animal

animal familier (n) (m)
pet

année/an (n) (f/m)
year

anniversaire (n) (m)
birthday

antenne (n) (f)
antenna

appareil photo (n) (m)
camera

apparence (n) (f)
appearance

appartement (n) (m)
apartment

après (prep)
after, past

après-midi (n) (m)
afternoon

araignée (n) (f)
spider

arbitre (n) (f)
referee

arbre (n) (m)
tree

arc-en-ciel (n) (m)
rainbow

B

arche (n) (f)
arch

argent (n) (m)
money, silver

argent de poche (n) (m)
pocket money

armée (n) (f)
army

armoire (n) (f)
wardrobe

arrêt d'autobus (n) (m)
bus stop

arrivée (n) (f)
arrival

arrosoir (n) (m)
watering can

art (n) (m)
art

artiste (n) (m/f)
artist

ascenseur (n) (m)
elevator

assez (adv)
enough

assiette (n) (f)
plate

assistant/assistante (n) (m/f)
assistant

assoiffé/assoiffée (adj)
thirsty

astronaute (n) (m/f)
astronaut

astronome (n) (m/f)
astronomer

athlétisme (n) (m)
athletics

atlas (n) (m)
atlas

au-dessous de (prep)
below

au-dessus de (prep)
above

aujourd'hui (adv)
today

aussi (adv)
also, too

autobus (n) (m)
bus

autocar (n) (m)
coach

autocollant (n) (m)
sticker

automne (n) (m)
autumn

autoroute (n) (f)
highway

autour (prep)
around

autre (adj)
other

avant (prep)
before

avec (prep)
with

avenir (n) (m)
future

aventure (n) (f)
adventure

avertissement (n) (m)
warning

avion (n) (m)
airplane, plane

avion à réaction (n) (m)
jet

avocat (n) (m)
avocado

babouin (n) (m)
baboon

badminton (n) (m)
badminton

bagages (n) (m)
luggage

bague (n) (f)
ring

baignoire (n) (f)
bathtub

baiser (n) (m)
kiss

balai (n) (m)
broom

balançoire (n) (f)
swing

balcon (n) (m)
balcony

baleine (n) (f)
whale

balle (n) (f)
ball

ballon (n) (m)
ball, balloon

ballon de soccer (n) (m)
soccer ball

banane (n) (f)
banana

banc (n) (m)
bench

bande (n) (f)
band

banque (n) (f)
bank (money)

barbe (n) (f)
beard

barbecue (n) (m)
barbecue

bas/basse (adj)
low

bas (n) (m)
sock

baseball (n) (m)
baseball

basketball (n) (m)
basketball

bataille (n) (f)
battle

bateau (n) (m)
boat

bateau à voiles (n) (m)
sailboat

bateau de pêche (n) (m)
fishing boat

bateau de sauvetage (n) (m)
lifeboat

bâtiment (n) (m)
building

bâton (n) (m)
bat (sports)

batterie (n) (f)
drum kit

beau/belle (adj)
handsome/beautiful

beaucoup (adv)
(a) lot

beau-père (n) (m)
stepfather

beauté (n) (f)
beauty

bébé (n) (m)
baby

bec (n) (m)
beak

belle-mère (n) (f)
stepmother

A
Ⓑ
Ⓒ
D
E
F
G
H
I
J
K
L
M
N
O
P
Q
R
S
T
U
V
W
X
Y
Z

bête (n) (f)
creature

beurre (n) (m)
butter

bibliothèque (n) (f)
library

bidon (n) (m)
can

bien (adj)
fine

bien (adv)
well

bientôt (adv)
soon

bienvenu/bienvenue (adj)
welcome

bijou (n) (m)
jewel

bijoux (n) (m)
jewellery

billes (n) (f)
marble (toy)

billet (n) (m)
note, ticket

biscuit (n) (m)
cookie

blague (n) (f)
joke

blanc/blanche (adj)
white

blé (n) (m)
wheat

blessure (n) (f)
injury

bleu/bleue (adj)
blue

blond/blonde (adj)
blonde

blouson (n) (m)
jacket

bois (n) (m)
wood

boisson (n) (f)
drink

boîte (n) (f)
box

boîte à lunch (n) (f)
lunch box

boîte aux lettres (n) (f)
mailbox

boîte d'allumettes (n) (f)
matchbox

bol (n) (m)
bowl (cereal)

bon/bonne (adj)
good

bonbon (n) (m)
candy

bondé/bondée (adj)
crowded

bonhomme de neige (n) (m)
snowman

bon marché (adj)
cheap

bord (n) (m)
edge

bord de la mer (n) (m)
seaside

botte (n) (f)
boot

bouche (n) (f)
mouth

bouchon (n) (m)
plug

boucle d'oreille (n) (f)
earring

boue (n) (f)
mud

bouée (n) (f)
buoy

boueux/boueuse (adj)
muddy

bougie (n) (f)
candle

bouilloire (n) (f)
kettle

boulangerie (n) (f)
bakery

boule de neige (n) (f)
snowball

boussole (n) (f)
compass

bouteille (n) (f)
bottle

bouton (n) (m)
button

bracelet (n) (m)
bracelet

branche (n) (f)
branch

bras (n) (m)
arm

brillant/brillante (adj)
bright, shiny

brise (n) (f)
breeze

brosse à cheveux (n) (f)
hairbrush

brosse à dents (n) (f)
toothbrush

brouette (n) (f)
wheelbarrow

brouillard (n) (m)
fog

brun (adj)
brown

bruyant/bruyante (adj)
loud, noisy

buée (n) (f)
steam

buisson (n) (m)
bush

bulbe (n) (m)
bulb (plant)

bulle (n) (f)
bubble

bureau (n) (m)
desk, office

bureau de poste (n) (m)
post office

but (n) (m)
goal

C

c'est
it's (it is)

cabane (n) (f)
hut

cacahuète (n) (f)
peanut

cache-cache (n) (m)
hide-and-seek

cadeau (n) (m)
gift, present

cadre (n) (m)
frame

café (n) (m)
café, coffee

cage (n) (f)
cage

cahier (n) (m)
exercise book

caisse (n) (f)
checkout

calculatrice (n) (f)
calculator

calendrier (n) (m)
calendar

calme (adj)
calm

camion (n) (m)
truck

camion de pompier
(n) (m)
fire engine

camionnette (n) (f)
van

campagne (n) (f)
countryside

canapé (n) (m)
sofa

canard (n) (m)
duck

caneton (n) (m)
duckling

canoé (n) (m)
canoe

cape (n) (f)
cloak

capitale (n) (f)
capital

capuchon (n) (m)
hood

carburant (n) (m)
fuel

carnet (n) (m)
notebook

carotte (n) (f)
carrot

carré (n) (m)
square

carrefour (n) (m)
crossing

carte (n) (f)
card, map, menu

carte d'anniversaire
(n) (f)
birthday card

carte postale (n) (f)
postcard

cartes (n) (f)
cards

carton (n) (m)
cardboard

casque (n) (m)
helmet

casquette (n) (f)
cap

cassé/cassée (adj)
broken

casse-tête (n) (m)
puzzle

casserole (n) (f)
saucepan

cave (n) (f)
cellar

CD (n) (m)
CD

ceinture (n) (f)
belt

célèbre (adj)
famous

celui-ci (pron)
this one

celui-là (pron)
that one

centre (n) (m)
centre

cercle (n) (m)
circle

céréale (n) (f)
cereal

cerf-volant (n) (m)
kite

certain/certaine (adj)
certain

cerveau (n) (m)
brain

cette nuit
tonight

chaîne (n) (f)
chain

chaise (n) (f)
chair

chaise longue (n) (f)
deck chair

chaleur (n) (f)
heat

chaloupe (n) (f)
rowboat

chambre (n) (f)
bedroom

chameau (n) (m)
camel

champ (n) (m)
field

champignon (n) (m)
mushroom

chanceux/chanceuse (adj)
lucky

chandail (n) (m)
sweater

changement (n) (m)
change

chant (n) (m)
singing

chapeau de soleil (n) (m)
sunhat

chaque (adj)
each

chariot (n) (m)
shopping cart

charrette (n) (f)
cart

chat (n) (m)
cat

château de sable (n) (m)
sandcastle

chaton (n) (m)
kitten

chaud/chaude (adj)
hot, warm

chaussure (n) (f)
shoe

chauve-souris (n) (f)
bat (animal)

chef (n) (m/f)
chef

chemin (n) (m)
path

cheminée (n) (f)
chimney

chemise (n) (f)
shirt

chemisier (n) (m)
blouse

chenille (n) (f)
caterpillar

cher/chère (adj)
dear, expensive

cheval (n) (m)
horse

chevalier (n) (m)
knight

cheveux (n) (m)
hair

cheville (n) (f)
ankle

chèvre (n) (f)
goat

chevreuil (n) (m)
deer

chien (n) (m)
dog

chien de berger (n) (m)
sheepdog

chimpanzé (n) (m)
chimpanzee

A B C D E F G H I J K L M N O P Q R S T U V W X Y Z

chiot (n) (m)
puppy

chirurgie (n) (f)
surgery

chocolat (n) (m)
chocolate

chocolat chaud (n) (m)
hot chocolate

chose (n) (f)
thing

chou (n) (m)
cabbage

ciel (n) (m)
sky

cil (n) (m)
eyelash

cinéma (n) (m)
movie theatre

cintre (n) (m)
coat hanger

circulation (n) (f)
traffic

cirque (n) (m)
circus

ciseaux (n) (m)
scissors

citron (n) (m)
lemon

citrouille (n) (f)
pumpkin

clair/claire (adj)
clear, light

clavier (n) (m)
keyboard

clé (n) (f)
key

client/cliente (n) (m/f)
customer

cloche (n) (f)
bell

clôture (n) (f)
fence

clown (n) (m)
clown

coccinelle (n) (f)
ladybug

cochon (n) (m)
pig

cochon d'Inde (n) (m)
guinea pig

code postal (n) (m)
postal code

cœur (n) (m)
heart

coffre à jouets (n) (m)
toy box

coiffeur/coiffeuse (n) (m/f)
hairdresser

coin (n) (m)
corner

collant/collante (adj)
sticky

collants (n) (m)
tights

colle (n) (f)
glue

collier (n) (m)
collar, necklace

colline (n) (f)
hill

coloré/colorée (adj)
colourful

comique (n) (m)
comic

commandes (n) (f)
controls

comme (prep)
like

comment (adv)
how

commode (n) (f)
chest of drawers

concert (n) (m)
concert

confiture (n) (f)
jam

confortable (adj)
comfortable

congélateur (n) (m)
freezer

content/contente (adj)
happy

continent (n) (m)
continent

contraire (n) (m)
opposite

coquillage (n) (m)
shell

corde (n) (f)
rope

corde à sauter (n) (f)
skipping rope

corne (n) (f)
horn

corps (n) (m)
body

côte (n) (f)
coast

coton (n) (m)
cotton

cou (n) (m)
neck

coucher de soleil (n) (m)
sunset

coude (n) (m)
elbow

couette (n) (f)
duvet

couleur (n) (f)
colour

couloir (n) (m)
hall

courageux/courageuse (adj)
brave

courbe (adj)
curved

couronne (n) (f)
crown

courriel (n) (m)
email

course (n) (f)
race

course à pied (n) (f)
running

courses (n) (f)
shopping

court/courte (adj)
short

cousin/cousine (n) (m/f)
cousin

coussin (n) (m)
cushion

couteau (n) (m)
knife

couvercle (n) (m)
lid

couverture (n) (f)
blanket

cow-boy (n) (m)
cowboy

crabe (n) (m)
crab

crapaud (n) (m)
toad

cravate (n) (f)
tie

crayon à mine (n) (m)
pencil

crayon de cire (n) (m)
crayon

crayon de couleur (n) (m)
coloured pencil

crème (n) (f)
cream

crème glacée (n) (f)
ice cream

crème solaire (n) (f)
suntan lotion

A
B
C
D
E
F
G
H
I
J
K
L
M
N
O
P
Q
R
S
T
U
V
W
X
Y
Z

crêpe (n) (f)
pancake

crocodile (n) (m)
crocodile

cruche (n) (f)
jug

cube (n) (m)
cube

cubes (n) (m)
toy blocks

cuillère (n) (f)
spoon

cuisine (n) (f)
kitchen

cuisinière (n) (f)
stove

curieux/curieuse (adj)
curious

cygne (n) (m)
swan

D

d'abord (adv)
first

d'habitude (adv)
usually

danger (n) (m)
danger

dangereux/dangereuse (adj)
dangerous

dans (prep)
into

danseur/danseuse (n) (m/f)
dancer

danseur/danseuse
de ballet (n) (m/f)
ballet dancer

date (n) (f)
date

dauphin (n) (m)
dolphin

de (prep)
from

dé/dés (n) (m)
dice

de l'autre côté de (prep)
across

débarbouillette (n) (f)
facecloth

décoration (n) (f)
decoration

défi (n) (m)
challenge

défilé (n) (m)
parade

dehors (adv)
outside

déjà (adv)
already

déjeuner (n) (m)
lunch

délicieux/délicieuse (adj)
delicious

deltaplane (n) (m)
hang-glider

demain (adv)
tomorrow

demi-cercle (n) (m)
semicircle

dent (n) (f)
tooth

dentifrice (n) (m)
toothpaste

dentiste (n) (m/f)
dentist

dernier/dernière (adj)
last

derrière (prep)
behind

désert (n) (m)
desert

désordre (n) (m)
mess

dessert (n) (m)
dessert

dessin (n) (m)
drawing (act of)

deux fois
twice

deuxième (adj)
second (2nd)

devoirs (n) (m)
homework

diagramme (n) (m)
diagram

dictionnaire (n) (m)
dictionary

Dieu (n) (m)
God

différent/différente (adj)
different

difficile (adj)
difficult

digital/digitale (adj)
digital

dindon (n) (m)
turkey

dîner (n) (m)
dinner

dinosaure (n) (m)
dinosaur

directement (adv)
directly

direction (n) (f)
direction

discothèque (n) (f)
disco

discours (n) (m)
speech

disparu(e) (adj)
extinct

disque dur (n) (m)
hard drive

distance (n) (f)
distance

divorcé/divorcée (adj)
divorced

doigt (n) (m)
finger

dôme (n) (m)
dome

dos (n) (m)
back (body)

douche (n) (f)
shower

dragon (n) (m)
dragon

drap (n) (m)
sheet (bed)

drapeau (n) (m)
flag

droit/droite (adj)
straight, right (not left)

dur/dure (adj)
hard, tough

DVD (n) (m)
DVD

eau (n) (f)
water

échange (n) (m)
exchange

échecs (n) (m)
chess

échelle (n) (f)
ladder

écho (n) (m)
echo

A
B
Ⓒ
Ⓓ
Ⓔ
F
G
H
I
J
K
L
M
N
O
P
Q
R
S
T
U
V
W
X
Y
Z

A
B
C
D
E
F
G
H
I
J
K
L
M
N
O
P
Q
R
S
T
U
V
W
X
Y
Z

éclair (n) (m)
lightning

école (n) (f)
school

écouteurs (n) (m)
headphones

écran (n) (m)
screen

écriture (n) (f)
writing (act of)

écureuil (n) (m)
squirrel

effet (n) (m)
effect

effrayé/effrayée (adj)
frightened

égal/égale (adj)
equal

église (n) (f)
church

élastique (n) (m)
rubber band

électrique (adj)
electrical

élégant/élégante (adj)
smart

éléphant (n) (m)
elephant

élève (n) (m/f)
pupil, student

elle (pron)
she

elles (pron)
they

émission (n) (f)
program (TV)

emploi (n) (m)
job

en arrière (adv)
backwards

en avant (adv)
forward

en bas (adv)
downstairs

en bois (adv)
wooden

en bonne santé
healthy

en colère
angry

en cuir
leather

en espèces
(in) cash

en face de (prep)
opposite

en forme
fit

en haut (adv)
upstairs

en plastique
plastic

en retard
late

en sécurité
safe

encore (adv)
again

encre (n) (f)
ink

encyclopédie (n) (f)
encyclopedia

endroit (n) (m)
place

enfant/enfants (n) (m/f)
child/children

ennui (n) (m)
trouble

ennuyeux/ennuyeuse (adj)
boring

ensemble (adv)
together

ensoleillé/ensoleillée (adj)
sunny

enthousiaste (adj)
enthusiastic

entre (prep)
between

entrée (n) (f)
entrance

enveloppe (n) (f)
envelope

environ (adv)
about

environnement (n) (m)
environment

épais/épaisse (adj)
thick

épaule (n) (f)
shoulder

éponge (n) (f)
sponge

épouse (n) (f)
wife

épuisette (n) (f)
net

équateur (n) (m)
equator

équipage (n) (m)
crew

équipe (n) (f)
team

équitation (n) (f)
horseback riding

erreur (n) (f)
mistake

escalier (n) (m)
stairs

escargot (n) (m)
snail

espace (n) (m)
space

espadrilles (n) (f)
running shoes

essence (n) (f)
gas (fuel)

essuie-tout (n) (m)
paper towel

est (n) (m)
east

estomac (n) (m)
stomach

et (conj)
and

étage (n) (m)
storey

étagère (n) (f)
shelf

étang (n) (m)
pond

été (n) (m)
summer

étoile (n) (f)
star

étoile de mer (n) (f)
starfish

étonnant/étonnante (adj)
surprising

étrange (adj)
strange

étranger/étrangère (adj)
foreign

être humain (n) (m)
human

étroit/étroite (adj)
narrow

événement (n) (m)
event

évier (n) (m)
sink (kitchen)

exact/exacte (adj)
right (correct)

examen (n) (m)
exam, test

excellent/excellente (adj)
excellent

excité/excitée (adj)
excited

exercice (n) (m)
exercise

expédition (n) (f)
expedition

expérience (n) (f)
experiment

expert/experte (n) (m/f)
expert

explorateur/exploratrice
(n) (m/f)
explorer

explosion (n) (f)
explosion

exposé (n) (m)
report (for school)

extrêmement (adv)
extremely

fabuleux/fabuleuse (adj)
fabulous

facile (adj)
easy

facteur/facteure (n) (m/f)
letter carrier, mailman,
postman

facture (n) (f)
bill

faible (adj)
faint (pale), weak

fait (n) (m)
fact

falaise (n) (f)
cliff

famille (n) (f)
family

fantastique (adj)
fantastic

farine (n) (f)
flour

fatigué/fatiguée (adj)
tired

faucon (n) (m)
hawk

fauteuil (n) (m)
armchair

fauteuil roulant (n) (m)
wheelchair

faux/fausse (adj)
false

femme (n) (f)
female (human), woman

fenêtre (n) (f)
window

fer à repasser (n) (m)
iron (clothes)

ferme (n) (f)
farm

fermé/fermée (adj)
closed

fermeture éclair (n) (f)
zipper

fermier/fermière (n) (m/f)
farmer

fête (n) (f)
festival, party

feu (n) (m)
fire

feuille (n) (f)
leaf

feutre (n) (m)
felt-tip pen

feux de signalisation
(n) (m)
traffic lights

ficelle (n) (f)
string

fille (n) (f)
daughter, girl

film (n) (m)
film

fils (n) (m)
son

fin (n) (f)
end (final part)

fin/fine (adj)
thin

fin de semaine (n) (f)
weekend

flèche (n) (f)
arrow

fleur (n) (f)
flower

flocon de neige (n) (m)
snowflake

flûte (n) (f)
flute

foin (n) (m)
hay

foire (n) (f)
fair

fond (n) (m)
bottom

forêt (n) (f)
forest

forêt tropicale (n) (f)
rainforest

forme (n) (f)
shape

formidable (adj)
great

fort/forte (adj)
strong

foulard (n) (m)
scarf

four (n) (m)
oven

fourchette (n) (f)
fork

fourmi (n) (f)
ant

frais/fraîche (adj)
cool, fresh

fraise (n) (f)
strawberry

framboise (n) (f)
raspberry

français (n) (m)
French

frère (n) (m)
brother

frisé/frisée (adj)
curly

frites (n) (f)
fries

froid/froide (adj)
cold

fromage (n) (m)
cheese

fruit (n) (m)
fruit

fumée (n) (f)
smoke

fusée (n) (f)
rocket, space rocket

A
B
C
D
E
F
G
H
I
J
K
L
M
N
O
P
Q
R
S
T
U
V
W
X
Y
Z

G

gagnant/gagnante (n) (m/f)
winner

galet (n) (m)
pebble

gant (n) (m)
glove

gant de cuisine (n) (m)
oven mitt

garage (n) (m)
garage

garçon (n) (m)
boy

gare (n) (f)
railway station, station

gâteau (n) (m)
cake

gâteau d'anniversaire (n) (m)
birthday cake

gauche (adj)
left

gaucher/gauchère (adj)
left-handed

gaz (n) (m)
gas

géant (n) (m)
giant

gelé/gelée (adj)
frozen

genou (n) (m)
knee

gens (n) (m)
people

gentil/gentille (adj)
kind (gentle)

gilet de sauvetage (n) (m)
life jacket

girafe (n) (f)
giraffe

glace (n) (f)
ice

glaçon (n) (m)
ice cube

glissade d'eau (n) (f)
waterslide

globe (n) (m)
globe

golf (n) (m)
golf

gomme à effacer (n) (f)
eraser

gomme à macher (n) (f)
chewing gum

gorille (n) (m)
gorilla

goutte (n) (f)
drop

gouvernement (n) (m)
government

graine (n) (f)
seed

grand/grande (adj)
big, tall

grand-mère (n) (f)
grandmother

grand-père (n) (m)
grandfather

grands-parents (n) (m)
grandparents

grange (n) (f)
barn

gratte-ciel (n) (m)
skyscraper

gratuit/gratuite (adj)
free (no cost)

grenier (n) (m)
attic

grenouille (n) (f)
frog

griffe (n) (f)
claw

grille-pain (n) (m)
toaster

gros/grosse (adj)
big, fat

grotte (n) (f)
cave

groupe (n) (m)
group

grue (n) (f)
crane

guépard (n) (m)
cheetah

guêpe (n) (f)
wasp

guerre (n) (f)
war

guide (n) (m)
guide

guitare (n) (f)
guitar

gymnastique (n) (f)
gymnastics

H

habitat (n) (m)
habitat

habitude (n) (f)
habit

hamster (n) (m)
hamster

hanche (n) (f)
hip

handicapé/handicapée (adj)
disabled

haricots (n) (m)
beans

haut (n) (m)
top

haut/haute (adj)
high

hélicoptère (n) (m)
helicopter (n)

hélicoptère de police (n) (m)
police helicopter

herbe (n) (f)
grass

héron (n) (m)
heron

héros/héroine (n) (m/f)
hero

heure (n) (f)
hour, time

heures d'ouverture (n) (f)
opening hours

hexagone (n) (m)
hexagon

hibou (n) (m)
owl

hier (adv)
yesterday

histoire (n) (f)
history, story

historique (adj)
historical

hiver (n) (m)
winter

hockey (n) (m)
hockey

hockey sur gazon (n) (m)
field hockey

homme (n) (m)
male (human), man

hôpital (n) (m)
hospital

horaire (n) (m)
timetable

horloge (n) (f)
clock

horrible (adj)
horrible

hors de (prep)
out of

hot-dog (n) (m)
hot dog

hôtel (n) (m)
hotel

huile (n) (f)
oil

I

idée (n) (f)
idea

il (pron)
he

île (n) (f)
island

illustration (n) (f)
illustration

ils/elles (pron)
they

image (n) (f)
picture

immobile (adj)
still

imperméable (n) (m)
raincoat

important/importante (adj)
important

impossible (adj)
impossible

incroyable (adj)
amazing

infirmière (n) (f)
nurse

information (n) (f)
information

ingrédient (n) (m)
ingredient

inhabituel/inhabituelle (adj)
unusual

injuste (adj)
unfair

inondation (n) (f)
flood

insecte (n) (m)
insect

insigne (n) (m)
badge

instruction (n) (f)
instruction

instrument (n) (m)
instrument

intelligent/intelligente (adj)
clever

intéressant/intéressante (adj)
interesting

international/
internationale (adj)
international

Internet (n) (m)
Internet

invitation (n) (f)
invitation

J

jamais (adv)
never

jambe (n) (f)
leg

jardin (n) (m)
garden

jardinier/jardinière
(n) (m/f)
gardener

jaune (adj)
yellow

je/j' (pron)
I

jean (n) (m)
jeans

jeu (n) (m)
game

jeu de plateau (n) (m)
board game

jeu électronique (n) (m)
computer game

jeu vidéo (n) (m)
video game (n)

jeune (adj)
young

Jeux olympiques
(n) (m)
Olympic Games

joli/jolie (adj)
pretty

jouet (n) (m)
toy

joueur/joueuse
(n) (m/f)
player

jour (n) (m)
day

journal (n) (m)
diary, newspaper

judo (n) (m)
judo

jumeau/jumelle (n) (m/f)
twin

jumelles (n) (f)
binoculars

jungle (n) (f)
jungle

jupe (n) (f)
skirt

jus (n) (m)
juice

jus d'orange (n) (m)
orange juice

jusqu'à (prep)
until

juste (adj)
correct

juste (adv)
just

K

kangourou (n) (m)
kangaroo

karaté (n) (m)
karate

koala (n) (m)
koala

L

la/lui/l' (pron)
her

là (adv)
there

là-bas (adv)
over there

lac (n) (m)
lake

A B C D E F G (H) (I) (J) (K) (L) M N O P Q R S T U V W X Y Z

A
B
C
D
E
F
G
H
I
J
K
Ⓛ
Ⓜ
N
O
P
Q
R
S
T
U
V
W
X
Y
Z

laid/laide (adj)
ugly

laine (n) (f)
wool

lait (n) (m)
milk

lait frappé (n) (m)
milkshake

laitier/laitière (adj)
dairy

laitue (n) (f)
lettuce

lampe (n) (f)
lamp

lampe de poche (n) (f)
flashlight

langue (n) (f)
language, tongue

lapin (n) (m)
rabbit

large (adj)
wide

lavabo (n) (m)
sink (bathroom)

le/lui/l' (pron)
him

le/la/l'/les (article)
the

le sien/la sienne (pron)
hers / his

leçon (n) (f)
lesson

lecteur de CD (n) (m)
CD player

lecteur de DVD (n) (m)
DVD player

lecteur MP3 (n) (m)
MP3 player

lecture (n) (f)
reading

léger/légère (adj)
light (not heavy)

légume (n) (m)
vegetable

lent/lente (adj)
slow

lentement (adv)
slowly

léopard (n) (m)
leopard

lettre (n) (f)
letter (alphabet, mail)

leur (adj)
their

lézard (n) (m)
lizard

libellule (n) (f)
dragonfly

liberté (n) (f)
freedom

librairie (n) (f)
bookstore

libre (adj)
free (not confined)

lièvre (n) (m)
hare

ligne (n) (f)
line

limonade (n) (f)
lemonade

lion (n) (m)
lion

lion de mer (n) (m)
sea lion (n)

liquide (n) (m)
liquid (n)

lisse (adj)
smooth

liste (n) (f)
list

liste de courses (n) (f)
shopping list

lit (n) (m)
bed

livre (n) (m)
book

loi (n) (f)
law

loin (adv)
far

long/longue (adj)
long

losange (n) (m)
diamond (shape)

loup (n) (m)
wolf

loupe (n) (f)
magnifying glass

lourd/lourde (adj)
heavy

lumière (n) (f)
light

lune (n) (f)
moon

lunettes (n) (f)
glasses

lunettes de natation (n) (f)
swim goggles

lunettes de soleil (n) (f)
sunglasses

machine (n) (f)
machine

machine à laver (n) (f)
washing machine

magasin (n) (m)
store

magazine (n) (m)
magazine

magicien/magicienne
(n) (m/f)
magician

magnétique (adj)
magnetic

maillot de bain
(n) (m)
bathing suit

main (n) (f)
hand

maintenant (adv)
now

mais (conj)
but

maison (n) (f)
home, house

maître/maîtresse
(n) (m/f)
teacher

mal de tête (n) (m)
headache

mal d'oreille (n) (m)
earache

malade (adj)
ill, sick

maladie (n) (f)
illness

maman (n) (f)
mom

mammifère (n) (m)
mammal

manche (n) (f)
sleeve

manteau (n) (m)
coat

maquillage (n) (m)
makeup

marché (n) (m)
market

marée (n) (f)
tide

marguerite (n) (f)
daisy

mari (n) (m)
husband

marié/mariée (adj)
married

marin (n) (m)
sailor

marionnette (n) (f)
puppet

masque (n) (m)
mask

match (n) (m)
match (sport)

matériel (n) (m)
equipment

mathématiques (n) (f)
math

matin (n) (m)
morning

mauvais/mauvaise (adj)
bad

mauvaise herbe (n) (f)
weed

me/moi/m' (pron)
me

médecin (n) (m)
doctor

médicament (n) (m)
medication

méduse (n) (f)
jellyfish

meilleur/meilleure (adj)
better

mélange (n) (m)
mixture

melon (n) (m)
melon

melon d'eau (n) (m)
watermelon

même (adv)
even

même (adj)
same

menton (n) (m)
chin

mer (n) (f)
sea

mère (n) (f)
mother

message (n) (m)
message

mesure (n) (f)
measurement

mètre-ruban (n) (m)
tape measure

métro (n) (m)
subway

meubles (n) (m)
furniture

micro-ondes (n) (m)
microwave

miel (n) (m)
honey

mieux (adj)
best

milieu (n) (m)
middle

mille
thousand

milliard
billion

million
million

minéral (n) (m)
mineral

minuit (n) (m)
midnight

minuscule (adj)
tiny

minute (n) (f)
minute

miroir (n) (m)
mirror

mitaine (n) (f)
mitten

mode (n) (f)
fashion

mois (n) (m)
month

moisson (n) (f)
harvest

moissonneuse-batteuse (n) (f)
combine harvester

moitié (n) (f)
half

mon/ma (adj)
my

monde (n) (m)
world

monstre (n) (m)
monster

montagne (n) (f)
mountain

montgolfière (n) (f)
hot-air balloon

montre (n) (f)
watch

moquette (n) (f)
carpet

morceau (n) (m)
piece

mort/morte (adj)
dead

mosquée (n) (f)
mosque

mot (n) (m)
term, word

moteur (n) (m)
motor

motif (n) (m)
pattern

moto (n) (f)
motorcycle

mou (adj)
soft

mouche (n) (f)
fly

mouchoir (n) (m)
handkerchief

mouette (n) (f)
seagull

mouillé/mouillée (adj)
wet

moustache (n) (f)
moustache, whisker

mouton (n) (m)
sheep

mur (n) (m)
wall

mûr/mûre (adj)
ripe

musée (n) (m)
museum

musicien/musicienne (n) (m/f)
musician

musique (n) (f)
music

n'importe qui (pron)
anybody

n'importe quoi (pron)
anything

nageoire (n) (f)
fin

natation (n) (f)
swimming

nature (n) (f)
nature

A
B
C
D
E
F
G
H
I
J
K
L
Ⓜ
Ⓝ
O
P
Q
R
S
T
U
V
W
X
Y
Z

A
B
C
D
E
F
G
H
I
J
K
L
M
(N)
(O)
(P)
Q
R
S
T
U
V
W
X
Y
Z

navire (n) (m)
ship

neige (n) (f)
snow

nénuphar (n) (m)
water lily

neveu (n) (m)
nephew

nez (n) (m)
nose

nid (n) (m)
nest

nièce (n) (f)
niece

Noël (n) (m)
Christmas

nœud (n) (m)
knot

noir/noire (adj)
black

nom (n) (m)
name

nombre (n) (m)
number

nord (n) (m)
north

notre (adj)
our

nouilles (n) (f)
noodles

nourriture (n) (f)
food

nous (pron)
we

nouveau/nouvelle (adj)
new

nouvelles (n) (f)
news

nuage (n) (m)
cloud

nuageux/nuageuse (adj)
cloudy

nuit (n) (f)
night

nulle part (adv)
nowhere

O

objet (n) (m)
object

occupé/occupée (adj)
busy

océan (n) (m)
ocean

odeur (n) (f)
smell

œil (n) (m)
eye

œuf (n) (m)
egg

oignon (n) (m)
onion

oiseau (n) (m)
bird

oiseau-mouche (n) (m)
hummingbird

oncle (n) (m)
uncle

ondulé/ondulée (adj)
wavy

ongle (n) (m)
nail

opération (n) (f)
operation

or (n) (m)
gold

orage (n) (m)
thunderstorm

orageux/orageuse (adj)
stormy

orange (adj)
orange (colour)

orange (n) (f)
orange (fruit)

orchestre (n) (m)
orchestra

ordinateur (n) (m)
computer

ordinateur portable
(n) (m)
laptop

ordures (n) (f)
garbage

oreille (n) (f)
ear

oreiller (n) (m)
pillow

orteil (n) (m)
toe

os (n) (m)
bone

ou (conj)
or

où (adv)
where

ouest (n) (m)
west

ouragan (n) (m)
hurricane

ours (n) (m)
bear

ours en peluche (n) (m)
teddy bear

ours polaire (n) (m)
polar bear

outil (n) (m)
tool

ouvert/ouverte (adj)
open

ovale (n) (m)
oval

P

page (n) (f)
page

paille (n) (f)
drinking straw, straw

pain (n) (m)
bread

paire (n) (f)
pair

paix (n) (f)
peace

palme (n) (f)
flipper

palmier (n) (m)
palm tree

panda (n) (m)
panda

panier (n) (m)
basket

panneau de signalisation
(n) (m)
sign

pantalon (n) (m)
pants

pantoufle (n) (f)
slipper

papa (n) (m)
dad

papier (n) (m)
paper

papier hygiénique (n) (m)
toilet paper

papiers-mouchoirs (n) (m)
tissues

papillon (n) (m)
butterfly

papillon de nuit (n) (m)
moth

parapluie (n) (m)
umbrella (for rain)

parasol (n) (m)
umbrella (for sun)

parc (n) (m)
park

parc d'attractions (n) (m)
fairground

parce que (conj)
because

parent (n) (m)
parent

paresseux/paresseuse (adj)
lazy

parfait/parfaite (adj)
perfect

particulier/particulière (adj)
special

partie (n) (f)
part

partout (adv)
everywhere

pas (n) (m)
step

passager/passagère (n) (m/f)
passenger

passé (n) (m)
past (history)

passeport (n) (m)
passport

passe-temps (n) (m)
hobby

pâte à modeler (n) (f)
modelling clay

pâtes (n) (f)
pasta

patient/patiente (adj)
patient

patient/patiente (n) (m/f)
patient

patinage sur glace (n) (m)
ice skating

patte (n) (f)
foot (animal), paw

pause (n) (f)
break

pauvre (adj)
poor

pays (n) (m)
country

peau (n) (f)
skin

pêche (n) (f)
fishing

pédale (n) (f)
pedal

peigne (n) (m)
comb

peinture (n) (f)
paint

pélican (n) (m)
pelican

pelle (n) (f)
spade

pelouse (n) (f)
lawn

pendant (prep)
during

pendant que (conj)
while

pentagone (n) (m)
pentagon

père (n) (m)
father

perle (n) (f)
bead

perroquet (n) (m)
parrot

personne (pron)
nobody

personne (n) (f)
person

personne âgée (n) (f)
old person

petit/petite (adj)
little, small

petit ami (m)
boyfriend

petit-déjeuner (n) (m)
breakfast

petit pain (m)
(bread) roll

petit tapis (m)
mat

petite amie (f)
girlfriend

peu profond/peu profonde (adj)
shallow

peut-être (adv)
maybe, perhaps

phare (n) (m)
lighthouse

pharmacie (n) (f)
drugstore

phoque (n) (m)
seal

photo (n) (f)
photo

piano (n) (m)
piano

pièce (n) (f)
room

pièce de monnaie (n) (f)
coin

pièce de théâtre (n) (f)
play (theatre)

pied (n) (m)
foot

pierre (n) (f)
stone

pile (n) (f)
battery

pilote (n) (m)
pilot

pin (n) (m)
pine tree

pinceau (n) (m)
paintbrush

pingouin (n) (m)
penguin

ping-pong (n) (m)
table tennis

pique-nique (n) (m)
picnic

pire (adj)
worst

piscine (n) (f)
swimming pool

pissenlit (n) (m)
dandelion

piste (n) (f)
runway

pizza (n) (f)
pizza

placard (n) (m)
cupboard

plafond (n) (m)
ceiling

plage (n) (f)
beach

planche à neige (n) (f)
snowboard

planche à roulettes (n) (f)
skateboard

planche de surf (n) (f)
surfboard

planète (n) (f)
planet

plante (n) (f)
plant

plat/plate (adj)
flat, level

plateau (n) (m)
tray

plein/pleine (adj)
full

plongée (n) (f)
diving

pluie (n) (f)
rain

plume (n) (f)
feather

A B C D E F G H I J K L M N O P Q R S T U V W X Y Z

A
B
C
D
E
F
G
H
I
J
K
L
M
N
O
(P)
(Q)
(R)
S
T
U
V
W
X
Y
Z

plus que (n)
more than

pneu (n) (m)
tire

poche (n) (f)
pocket

pochette (n) (f)
pouch

poêle (n) (f)
frying pan

poils (n) (m)
fur

poilu/poilue (adj)
hairy

point (n) (m)
point

poire (n) (f)
pear

pois (m)
pea

poisson (n) (m)
fish

poisson rouge (n) (m)
goldfish

poitrine (n) (f)
chest

poivre (n) (m)
pepper

polar (n) (m)
fleece

poli/polie (adj)
polite

police (n) (f)
police

policier/policière (n) (f)
police officer

pomme (n) (f)
apple

pomme de pin (n) (f)
pine cone

pomme de terre (n) (f)
potato

pompier (n) (m)
firefighter

pont (n) (m)
bridge, deck (boat)

populaire (adj)
popular

port (n) (m)
harbour

porte (n) (f)
door

porte d'entrée (n) (f)
front door

porte-monnaie (n) (m)
wallet

possible (adj)
possible

poste (n) (f)
mail

pot de peinture (n) (m)
paint can

poteau (n) (m)
pole

poubelle (n) (f)
garbage can

pouce (n) (m)
thumb

poudre (n) (f)
powder

poulet (n) (m)
chicken

poupée (n) (f)
doll

pourquoi (adv)
why

poussette (n) (f)
stroller

poussière (n) (f)
dust

poussin (n) (m)
chick

préféré/préférée (adj)
favourite

premier/première (adj)
first

premiers soins (n) (m)
first aid

près de (prep)
near

présentation (n) (f)
introduction

président/e (n) (m/f)
president

presque (adv)
almost, nearly

prêt/prête (adj)
ready

prince (n) (m)
prince

princesse (n) (f)
princess

principal/principale (adj)
main

printemps (n) (m)
spring (season)

prise électrique (n) (f)
plug (electric)

prix (n) (m)
price, prize

probablement (adv)
probably

problème (n) (m)
problem

prochain/prochaine (adj)
next

proche (adj)
close (near)

profond/profonde (adj)
deep

projet (n) (m)
project

promenade (n) (f)
walk

propre (adj)
clean, own

prudent/prudente (adj)
careful

punaise (n) (f)
thumb tack

pyjama (n) (m)
pyjamas

quand (adv)
when

quart (n) (m)
quarter

quelque chose (pron)
something

quelquefois (adv)
sometimes

quelques (adj)
some

quelqu'un (pron)
someone

question (n) (f)
question

queue (n) (f)
lineup, tail

qui (pron)
who

quiz (n) (m)
quiz

racine (n) (f)
root

radio (n) (f)
radio

raide (adj)
steep

raisin (n) (m)
grape

rame (n) (f)
oar

rapide (adj)
fast

raquette (n) (f)
racquet

rat (n) (m)
rat

râteau (n) (m)
rake

rayures (n) (f)
stripes

recette (n) (f)
recipe

récolte (n) (f)
crop

récompense (n) (f)
reward

récréation (n) (f)
playtime

rectangle (n) (m)
rectangle

reçu (n) (m)
receipt

réel/réelle (adj)
real

réfrigérateur (n) (m)
fridge

région (n) (f)
area

règle (n) (f)
ruler (measuring)

reine (n) (f)
queen

religion (n) (f)
religion

renard (n) (m)
fox

repas (n) (m)
meal

réponse (n) (f)
answer

requin (n) (m)
shark

restaurant (n) (m)
restaurant

rêve (n) (m)
dream

réveil (n) (m)
alarm clock

réverbère (n) (m)
street light

rhinocéros (n) (m)
rhinoceros

riche (adj)
rich

rideau (n) (m)
curtain

rien (pron)
nothing

rive (n) (f)
bank (river)

rivière (n) (f)
river

riz (n) (m)
rice

robe (n) (f)
dress

robinet (n) (m)
tap (faucet)

robot (n) (m)
robot

roche (n) (f)
rock

roi (n) (m)
king

rond/ronde (adj)
round

rose (adj)
pink

rose (n) (f)
rose

roue (n) (f)
wheel

rouge (adj)
red

route (n) (f)
road

ruban (n) (m)
ribbon

ruche (n) (f)
hive

rue (n) (f)
street

rugby (n) (m)
rugby

rugueux/rugueuse (adj)
rough

S

s'il te plaît
please

sable (n) (m)
sand

sac (n) (m)
bag, sack, shopping bag

sac à dos (n) (m)
backpack

sac à main (n) (m)
purse

sac de couchage (n) (m)
sleeping bag

sac d'école (n) (m)
school bag

sac en plastique (n) (m)
plastic bag

saison (n) (f)
season

salade (n) (f)
salad

salaire (n) (m)
pay

sale (adj)
dirty

salle à manger (n) (f)
dining room

salle de bains (n) (f)
bathroom

salle de classe (n) (f)
classroom

salon (n) (m)
living room

salut
hi

sandale (n) (f)
sandal

sandwich (n) (m)
sandwich

sang (n) (m)
blood

sans (prep)
without

sauterelle (n) (f)
grasshopper

savon (n) (m)
soap

scarabée (n) (m)
beetle

sciences (n) (f)
science

scientifique (n) (m/f)
scientist

seau (n) (m)
bucket

sec/sèche (adj)
dry

seconde (n) (f)
second (time)

secours (n) (m)
rescue

sel (n) (m)
salt

selle (n) (f)
saddle

semaine (n) (f)
week

sens (n) (m)
meaning

séparément (adv)
apart

A B C D E F G H I J K L M N O P Q R S T U V W X Y Z

A
B
C
D
E
F
G
H
I
J
K
L
M
N
O
P
Q
R
(S)
(T)
U
V
W
X
Y
Z

serpent (n) (m)
snake

serre (n) (f)
greenhouse

serré/serrée (adj)
tight

serveur (n) (m)
waiter

serveuse (n) (f)
waitress

serviette (n) (f)
towel

seul/seule (adj)
alone

seulement (adv)
only

sévère (adj)
strict

shampooing (n) (m)
shampoo

short (n) (m)
shorts

sifflement (n) (m)
whistle

silencieux/silencieuse (adj)
quiet

singe (n) (m)
monkey

site web (n) (m)
website

ski (n) (m)
skiing

soccer (n) (m)
soccer

sœur (n) (f)
sister

soir (n) (m)
evening

sol (n) (m)
floor

soleil (n) (m)
sun

solide (n) (m)
solid

sombre (adj)
dark

son/sa (adj)
her/his/its

sorte (n) (f)
kind (type)

sortie (n) (f)
exit

souhait (n) (m)
wish

sourcil (n) (m)
eyebrow

sourd/sourde (adj)
deaf

souris (n) (f)
mouse (animal, computer)

sous (prep)
under

sous-marin (n) (m)
submarine

sous-vêtements (n) (m)
underwear

souvent (adv)
often

spaghettis (n) (m)
spaghetti

spectacle (n) (m)
show

sport (n) (m)
sport

squelette (n) (m)
skeleton

stupide (adj)
stupid

stylo (n) (m)
pen

sucre (n) (m)
sugar

sud (n) (m)
south

sujet (n) (m)
subject

supermarché (n) (m)
supermarket

supplémentaire (adj)
extra

sur (prep)
about, on top of

sûr/sûre (adj)
sure

surf (n) (m)
surfing

surface (n) (f)
surface

surprise (n) (f)
surprise

surveillant de baignade (n) (m)
lifeguard

sympathique (adj)
nice

table (n) (f)
table

tableau (n) (m)
picture

tableau noir (n) (m)
blackboard

tablier (n) (m)
apron

taille (n) (f)
size, waist

tante (n) (f)
aunt

tapis (n) (m)
rug

tapis de souris (n) (m)
mouse pad

tasse (n) (f)
cup, mug

taxi (n) (m)
taxi

tee-shirt (n) (m)
T-shirt

télécommande (n) (f)
remote control

téléphone (n) (m)
phone

téléphone cellulaire (n) (m)
cellphone

télescope (n) (m)
telescope

télévision (n) (f)
television

temps (n) (m)
weather

temps libre (n) (m)
free time

tennis (n) (m)
tennis

tente (n) (f)
tent

terrain (n) (m)
land

terrain de jeu (n) (m)
playground

Terre (n) (f)
Earth (planet)

terre (n) (f)
ground, soil

terrible (adj)
terrible

têtard (n) (m)
tadpole

tête (n) (f)
head

texto (n) (m)
text message

thé (n) (m)
tea

thermomètre (n) (m)
thermometer

tige (n) (f)
stem

tigre (n) (m)
tiger

timbre (n) (m)
stamp

timide (adj)
shy

tiroir (n) (m)
drawer

tissu (n) (m)
cloth

toilettes (n) (f)
toilet

toit (n) (m)
roof

tomate (n) (f)
tomato

tondeuse à gazon (n) (f)
lawn mower

torchon (n) (m)
dish towel

tornade (n) (f)
tornado

tortue (n) (f)
tortoise

tortue de mer (n) (f)
turtle

tôt (adv)
early

toucan (n) (m)
toucan

toujours (adv)
always

touriste (n) (m/f)
tourist

tournant (n) (m)
turn (bend)

tournesol (n) (m)
sunflower

tourniquet (n) (m)
carousel

tous (adj)
every

tous les jours (adv)
everyday

tout (pron)
everything

tout/toute (adj)
all

tout à coup (adv)
suddenly

tout de suite (adv)
immediately

tout le monde (pron)
everybody

toux (n) (f)
cough

tracteur (n) (m)
tractor

train (n) (m)
train, train set

traîneau (n) (m)
sleigh

trajet (n) (m)
route

tranquille (adj)
peaceful

tranquillement (adv)
quietly

transplantoir (n) (m)
trowel

transport (n) (m)
transport

traversier (n) (m)
ferry

très (adv)
very

triangle (n) (m)
triangle

triste (adj)
sad

troisième (adj)
third

trombone (n) (m)
paper clip

trompe (n) (f)
trunk (animal)

tronc (n) (m)
trunk (tree)

tropical/tropicale (adj)
tropical

trottoir (n) (m)
sidewalk

trou (n) (m)
hole

troupeau (n) (m)
flock (of sheep)

trousse (n) (f)
pencil case

tu/vous (pron)
you

tube (n) (m)
tube

tunnel (n) (m)
tunnel

tuque (n) (f)
toque

U

un/une (article)
a, an

uniforme (n) (m)
uniform

uniforme scolaire (n) (m)
school uniform

univers (n) (m)
universe

urgence (n) (f)
emergency

usine (n) (f)
factory

utile (adj)
useful

V

vacances (n) (f)
holiday, vacation

vache (n) (f)
cow

vague (n) (f)
wave

valise (n) (f)
suitcase

veau (n) (m)
calf

vedette de cinéma (n) (f)
film star

végétarien/végétarienne
(n) (m/f)
vegetarian

vélo (n) (m)
bike

vélo de montagne (n) (m)
mountain bike

vendeur/vendeuse
(n) (m/f)
sales person

vent (n) (m)
wind

venteux
windy

ventre (n) (m)
tummy

ver (n) (m)
worm

A
B
C
D
E
F
G
H
I
J
K
L
M
N
O
P
Q
R
S
T
U
(V)
W
X
(Y)
(Z)

ver de terre (n) (m)
earthworm

verbe (n) (m)
verb

verre (n) (m)
glass (drink)

vers (prep)
toward

vert/verte (adj)
green

vêtements (n) (m)
clothes

vétérinaire (n) (m/f)
vet

viande (n) (f)
meat

vide (adj)
empty

vie (n) (f)
life

vieux/vieille (adj)
old

vilain/vilaine (adj)
naughty

ville (n) (f)
city, town

violet/violette (adj)
purple

violon (n) (m)
violin

visage (n) (m)
face

vite (adv)
quickly

voile (n) (f)
sail

voisin/voisine (n) (m/f)
neighbour

voiture (n) (f)
car

voiture de course (n) (f)
race car

voiture de police (n) (f)
police car

voix (n) (f)
voice

votre (adj)
your

voyage (n) (m)
journey, trip

vrai/vraie (adj)
true

vraiment (adv)
really

yacht (n) (m)
yacht

yogourt (n) (m)
yogourt

zèbre (n) (m)
zebra

zone (n) (f)
zone

zoo (n) (m)
zoo

Speaking French

In this dictionary, we have spelled out each French word in a way that will help you pronounce it. Use this guide to help you understand how the word should sound when you say it. Some French words look the same as English, but sound very different!

Letter	Pronunciation	Our spelling	Example
a, à, â	between the *a* in h*a*t and f*a*r	*a* or *ah*	**adresse** *a-dreys*
ch	like *sh* in *sh*ip	*sh*	**changer** *shahn-zhay*
ç	like *s* in *s*it	*s*	**garçon** *gar-so(n)*
é	like *ay* in d*ay*	*ay*	**café** *ka-fay*
è, ê	like *e* in *e*t	*eh*	**crème** *krehm*
e	like *er* in oth*er*	*uh*	**de** *duh*
gn	like the *ni* in o*ni*on	*nye*	**ligne** *leen-ye*
i, y	like *ee* in f*ee*t	*ee*	**fille** *fee-ye*
j, and sometimes g	like *s* in mea*s*ure	*zh*	**bonjour** *bon-zhoor*
qu	like *k* in *k*ing	*k*	**queue** *kuh*
o, ô	like *o* in m*o*re	*o* or *oh*	**porte** *port*
r	say *ruh* at the back of your throat, as if you're gargling	*r*	**fleur** *fluhr*
u	like *ew* in f*ew*	*ew*	**tu** *tew*
an, en, ien, in, ain, ein, on, un am, em, im, aim, eim, om, um	the *n* is not pronounced, but the vowel in front of it should have a nasal sound, as if the word ended in *ng*. For example, as if you said *song*, but stopped before saying the final *ng*.	*a(n), ah(n), o(n)*	**bien** *bya(n)*

Verbs

This section gives a list of useful verbs (doing words). You have the infinitive (to...) of the verb. The most useful verbs, such as "to be" *être* and "to have" *avoir*, are written out so that you can see how they change depending on who is doing the action. I = je, you = tu, he/she = il/elle, we = nous, you (plural and formal) = vous, and they = ils/elles.

We have also written out three of the most regular French verbs: to give = *donner*, to finish = *finir* and to sell = *vendre*, so you can see how these change.

There is also a reflexive verb written out. Reflexive verbs are often used where you would say "myself" or "yourself" in English. An example is: to wash oneself = *se laver*.

The verbs that are written out are shown in the present tense—they describe what is happening now.

to act
faire du théâtre
fair dew tay-a-truh

to agree
être d'accord
eh-truh da-kor

to allow
permettre
pair-met-truh

to appear
apparaître
ap-par-eh-truh

to ask
demander
duh-mahn-day

to bake
faire de la pâtisserie
fair duh la paht-eess-ree

to bark
aboyer
ab-wa-yay

to be
être
eh-truh
I am
je suis
zhuh swee
you are
tu es
tew ay
he/she is
il/elle est
eel/ehl ay
we are
nous sommes
noo sum
you (plural) are
vous êtes
voos eht
they are
ils/elles sont
eel/ehl so(n)

to be able
pouvoir
poov-wahr

to be born
être né
eh-truh nay

to be called
être appelé
eh-truh ap-play

to be cold
avoir froid
av-wahr frwa

to be hungry
avoir faim
av-wahr fa(m)

to be scared of
avoir peur de
av-wahr puhr duh

to be thirsty
avoir soif
av-wahr swaf

to become
devenir
duh-vuh-neer

Je fais de la pâtisserie.
I am baking.

Simon **croque** une pomme.
Simon **bites** an apple.

Elle **gonfle** un ballon.
She **blows** up a balloon.

Luc **nettoie** le sol.
Luc **cleans** the floor.

to begin
commencer
kom-ahn-say

to behave
se comporter
suh kom-por-tay

to believe
croire
krwahr

to bend
plier
plee-yay

to bird-watch
observer les oiseaux
ob-zair-vay layz wa-zoh

to bite
croquer
kro-kay

to block
bloquer
blo-kay

to blow
gonfler
gon-flay

to boil
bouillir
boo-yeer

to borrow
emprunter
ahm-pran-tay

to bounce
rebondir
ruh-bon-deer

to brake
freiner
fray-nay

to break
casser
kah-say

to breathe
respirer
ruh-speer-ay

to bring
apporter
ap-por-tay

to brush
brosser
bros-say

to brush one's teeth
se brosser les dents
suh bros-say lay dah(n)

to build
construire
kon-strweer

to bump into
rentrer dans
rahn-tray dah(n)

to buy
acheter
ash-tay

to camp
camper
kahm-pay

to carry
porter
por-tay

to catch
attraper
at-tra-pay

to cause
causer
koh-zay

to celebrate
célébrer
say-lay-bray

to change
changer
shahn-zhay

to charge (a phone)
recharger
ruh-shar-zhay

to check
vérifier
vair-eef-yay

to choose
choisir
shwa-zeer

to clean
nettoyer
net-wa-yay

to clear (a table)
débarrasser
day-bar-ra-say

to climb
grimper
gram-pay

to close
fermer
fair-may

Attrape le ballon !
Catch the ball!

115

to collect
collectionner
kol-lek-syo-nay

to come
venir
vuh-neer

to come back
revenir
ruh-vuh-neer

to come from
venir de
vuh-neer duh

to compare
comparer
kom-pa-ray

to complain
se plaindre
suh plan-druh

to contain
contenir
kon-tuh-neer

to continue
continuer
kon-teen-ew-ay

to cook
cuisiner
kwee-zee-nay

to copy
copier
kop-yay

to cost
coûter
koo-tay

to count
compter
kom-tay

to cover
couvrir
koov-reer

to crack
craquer
kra-kay

to crash
s'écraser
say-krah-zay

to create
créer
kray-ay

to cross
traverser
tra-vair-say

to cry
pleurer
pluhr-ay

to cut
couper
koo-pay

to cut out
découper
day-koo-pay

to cycle
faire du vélo
fair dew vay-lo

to dance
danser
dahn-say

to decide
décider
day-see-day

to decorate
décorer
day-ko-ray

to describe
décrire
day-kreer

to destroy
détruire
day-trweer

to die
mourir
moo-reer

to dig
creuser
kruh-zay

to disappear
disparaître
dees-par-eh-truh

to discover
découvrir
day-koov-reer

Marie **danse** bien.
Marie **dances** well.

Caroline **creuse** dans le sable.
Caroline **digs** in the sand.

116

Stéphane dessine.
Stéphane draws.

to dive
plonger
plon-jay

to do
faire
fair
I do
je fais
zhuh fay
you do
tu fais
tew fay
he/she does
il/elle fait
eel/ehl fay
we do
nous faisons
noo feh-zho(n)
you (plural) do
vous faites
voo feht
they do
ils/elles font
eel/ehl fo(n)

to draw
dessiner
dess-ee-nay

to dream
rêver
reh-vay

to dress up
s'habiller
sa-bee-yay

to drink
boire
bwahr

to drive
conduire
kon-dweer

to dry
sécher
say-shay

to earn
gagner
gan-yay

to eat
manger
mahn-zhay

to encourage
encourager
ahn-koo-ra-zhay

to enjoy
aimer
eh-may

to escape
s'échapper
say-shap-pay

to explain
expliquer
eks-plee-kay

to explode
exploser
ek-sploh-zay

to face
affronter
af-fron-tay

to fall
tomber
tom-bay

to fall down
s'écrouler
say-kroo-lay

to feed
nourrir
noo-reer

to feel
ressentir
ruh-sahn-teer

to fetch
aller chercher
al-lay shair-shay

to fight
se battre
suh bat-truh

to fill
remplir
rahm-pleer

to find
trouver
troo-vay

to find out
se renseigner sur
suh rahn-sen-yay soor

Je **mange** du gâteau au chocolat.
I **eat** some chocolate cake.

Il faut **nourrir** les chiens !
We need to **feed** the dogs!

117

to finish
finir
feen-eer
I finish
je finis
zhuh feen-ee
you finish
tu finis
tew feen-ee
he/she finishes
il/elle finit
eel/ehl feen-ee
we finish
nous finissons
noo feen-ee-so(n)
you finish
vous finissez
voo feen-ee-say
they finish
ils/elles finissent
eel/ehl feen-eess

to float
flotter
flot-tay

to fly
voler
vo-lay

to fold
plier
plee-yay

to follow
suivre
sweev-ruh

to forget
oublier
oo-blee-yay

Plie le papier.
Fold the paper.

to freeze
geler
zhuh-lay

to frighten
effrayer
eh-fray-yay

to garden
jardiner
zhar-dee-nay

to get
recevoir
ruh-suhv-wahr

to get on (a bus)
monter
mon-tay

to get ready
se préparer
suh pray-pa-ray

to get up
se lever
suh le-vay

to give
donner
don-nay
I give
je donne
zhuh dunn
you give
tu donnes
tew dunn
he/she gives
il/elle donne
eel/ehl dunn
we give
nous donnons
noo dunn-o(n)
you (plural) give
vous donnez
voo dunn-ay
they give
ils/elles donnent
eel/ehl dunn

to go
aller
ah-lay
I go
je vais
zhuh vay
you go
tu vas
tew vah
he/she goes
il/elle va
eel/ehl vah
we go
nous allons
noos ah-lo(n)
you (plural) go
vous allez
voos ah-lay
they go
ils/elles vont
eel/ehl vo(n)

to go camping
faire de camping
fair dew kahm-peeng

to go on holiday/vacation
partir en vacances
par-teer ah(n) vak-ahns

to go out
sortir
sor-teer

Bruno **prend** des œufs pour le petit-déjeuner.
Bruno **has** eggs for breakfast.

to go shopping
faire les courses
fair lay koorss

to go to the movies
aller au cinéma
ah-lay oh see-nay-ma

to grow
pousser
poo-say

to guess
deviner
duh-vee-nay

to hang up (a phone)
raccrocher
rak-ro-shay

to happen
arriver
ar-ree-vay

to hate
détester
day-tes-tay

to have
avoir
av-wahr
I have
j'ai
zhay
you have
tu as
tew ah
he/she has
il/elle a
eel/ehl ah
we have
nous avons
noos av-o(n)
you (plural) have
vous avez
voos av-ay
they have
ils/elles ont
eel/ehl o(n)

to have a shower
prendre une douche
prahn-druh ewn doosh

to have breakfast
prendre le petit-déjeuner
prahn-druh luh puh-tee day-zhuh-nay

Sophie s'amuse !
Sophie has fun!

to have fun
s'amuser
sam-ew-zay

to have to
devoir
duhv-wahr

to hear
entendre
ahn-tahn-druh

to help
aider
eh-day

to hide
cacher
ka-shay

to hit
frapper
frap-pay

to hold
tenir
tuh-neer

to hop
sauter
soh-tay

to hope
espérer
es-pair-ay

to hurry
se dépêcher
suh day-peh-shay

to hurt
blesser
bless-ay

to imagine
imaginer
ee-ma-zhee-nay

to include
inclure
an-klewr

to inspire
inspirer
an-spee-ray

to invent
inventer
an-vahn-tay

to invite
inviter
an-vee-tay

to join
joindre
zhwan-druh

to jump
sauter
soh-tay

to keep
garder
gar-day

to kick
donner un coup de pied
don-nay a(n) koo duh pyay

to kill
tuer
tew-ay

to kiss
embrasser
ahm-bra-say

to know (someone)
connaître
kon-neh-truh

to know (something)
savoir
sav-wahr

Les grenouilles sautent haut.
The frogs jump high.

119

to land (in a plane) • atterrir

to land (in a plane)
atterrir
at-tair-eer

to last
durer
dew-ray

to laugh
rire
reer

to leap
bondir
bon-deer

to learn
apprendre
ap-prahn-druh

to lie
mentir
mahn-teer

to lift
lever
luh-vay

to like
aimer
eh-may

to listen to
écouter
ay-koo-tay

to live
vivre
veev-ruh

to lock
fermer à clé
fair-may ah klay

to look
regarder
ruh-gar-day

to look after
s'occuper de
sok-ew-pay duh

to look for
chercher
shair-shay

to lose
perdre
pair-druh

to love
aimer
eh-may

to magnify
grossir
groh-seer

to make
fabriquer
fab-ree-kay

to make a wish
faire un vœu
fair a(n) vuh

to make friends
se faire des amis
suh fair dez a-mee

Lucie **ouvre** la porte.
*Lucie **opens** the door.*

to marry
se marier
suh mar-yay

to mean
signifier
seen-yeef-yay

to meet
rencontrer
rahn-kon-tray

to move
bouger
boo-zhay

to need
avoir besoin de
av-wahr buh-zwah(n) duh

to not feel well
ne pas se sentir bien
nuh pah suh sahn-teer bya(n)

to notice
remarquer
ruh-mar-kay

to offer
offrir
off-reer

to open
ouvrir
oov-reer

to own
posséder
po-say-day

Emma **rit** !
*Emma **laughs**!*

Charlotte **regarde** de la terre.
*Charlotte **looks** at some earth.*

to pack
faire les valises
fair lay val-eez

to paint
peindre
pan-druh

to pay
payer
pay-yay

to persuade
persuader
pair-swa-day

to pick up
ramasser
ram-ah-say

to plan
organiser
or-gan-ee-zay

to play
jouer
zhoo-ay

to play an instrument
jouer d'un instrument
zhoo-ay dune ahn-stre-mahn

to point
indiquer
an-dee-kay

to pour
verser
vair-say

to practise
s'entraîner
sahn-treh-nay

to predict
prédire
pray-deer

to prefer
préférer
pray-fair-ay

to prepare
préparer
pray-pa-ray

to press
appuyer sur
ap-pwee-yay soor

to pretend
faire semblant
fair sahm-blah(n)

to print
imprimer
am-pree-may

to produce
produire
pro-dweer

to promise
promettre
pro-met-truh

to protect
protéger
pro-tay-zhay

to provide
fournir
foor-neer

to pull
tirer
teer-ay

to push
pousser
poo-say

to put
mettre
met-truh

to put away
ranger
rahn-zhay

to rain
pleuvoir
pluhv-wahr

to reach
atteindre
at-tan-druh

Verse l'eau doucement !
Pour the water carefully!

Peux-tu **peindre** un tableau ?
Can you **paint** a picture?

to read
lire
leer

to realize
se rendre compte
suh rahn-druh komt

to recognize
reconnaître
ruh-kon-neh-truh

to refuse
refuser
ruh-few-zay

to relax
se détendre
suh day-tahn-druh

to remain
rester
res-tay

to remember
se souvenir de
suh soo-vuh-neer duh

to repair
réparer
ray-pa-ray

to rest
se reposer
suh ruh-poh-zay

to return
revenir
ruh-vuh-neer

Mathieu **court** vite.
Mathieu **runs** quickly.

to ride a bike
faire du vélo
fair dew vay-lo

to ride a horse
monter à cheval
mon-tay ah shuh-val

to ring
sonner
so-nay

to roll
rouler
roo-lay

to rollerblade
faire du patin à roues alignées
fair dew pa-ta(n) ah roo ah-lin-yay

to row
ramer
ra-may

to rub
frotter
fro-tay

to run
courir
koo-reer

to run after
poursuivre
poor-swee-vruh

to sail
faire de la voile
fair duh la vwal

to save
sauver
soh-vay

to say
dire
deer

to score (a goal)
marquer
mar-kay

to scratch (oneself)
se gratter
suh grat-tay

to search
chercher
shair-shay

to see
voir
vwahr

to seem
sembler
sahm-blay

Mélanie **monte à cheval**.
Mélanie **rides a horse**.

Julie **lit** son livre.
Julie **reads** her book.

to sell
vendre
vahn-druh
I sell
je vends
zhuh vah(n)
you sell
tu vends
tew vah(n)
he/she sells
il/elle vend
eel/ehl vah(n)
we sell
nous vendons
noo vah(n)-doh(n)
you (plural) sell
vous vendez
voo vah(n)-day
they sell
ils/elles vendent
eel/ehl vah(n)d

to send
envoyer
ahn-vwa-yay

to set a table
mettre la table
met-truh la tab-luh

to share
partager
par-ta-zhay

to shine
briller
bree-yay

to shout
crier
kree-yay

Clément **dort**.
Clément is sleeping.

to show
montrer
mon-tray

to sing
chanter
shahn-tay

to sit
s'asseoir
sass-wahr

to skate (on ice)
patiner (sur glace)
pa-tee-nay

to ski
skier
skee-yay

to sleep
dormir
dor-meer

to slide
glisser
glee-say

to slip
glisser
glee-say

to smell
sentir
sahn-teer

to smile
sourire
soo-reer

to snow
neiger
nay-zhay

Léa **crie** après son amie.
Léa **shouts** at her friend.

to sound (like)
sembler
sahm-blay

to speak
parler
par-lay

to spell
épeler
ay-puh-lay

to spin
tourner
toor-nay

to spread
étaler
ay-ta-lay

to stand
se tenir debout
suh tuh-neer duh-boo

to stand up
se lever
suh luh-vay

to start
commencer
kom-ahn-say

to stay
rester
res-tay

to stick
coller
kol-lay

Étale le chocolat sur les gâteaux.
Spread the chocolate on the cakes.

*La fille **prend une photo.***
The girl takes a photo.

to sting
piquer
pee-kay

to stop
arrêter
arh-reh-tay

to stretch
s'étirer
say-teer-ay

to study
étudier
ay-tewd-yay

to surf
surfer
soor-fay

to surprise
surprendre
soor-prahn-druh

to survive
survivre
soor-veev-ruh

to swim
nager
na-zhay

to take
prendre
prahn-druh

to take a photo
prendre une photo
prahn-druh ewn fo-toh

to take away
emporter
ahm-por-tay

to take turns
faire à tour de rôle
fair ah toor duh rohl

to talk
parler
par-lay

to taste
goûter
goo-tay

to teach
enseigner
ahn-sen-yay

to tease
taquiner
tak-ee-nay

to tell
raconter
rak-on-tay

to tell a story
raconter une histoire
rak-on-tay ewn eest-wahr

to tell the time
dire l'heure
deer luhr

to thank
remercier
ruh-mair-syay

to think
réfléchir
ray-flay-sheer

*Valérie **réfléchit.***
Valérie is thinking.

to throw
jeter
zhuh-tay

to tidy up
ranger
rahn-zhay

to tie
attacher
at-ta-shay

to touch
toucher
too-shay

to train
entraîner
ahn-treh-nay

to translate
traduire
trad-weer

to travel
voyager
vwa-ya-zhay

to treat (well)
traiter (bien)
tray-tay bya(n)

to try (on)
essayer
es-say-yay

to turn
tourner
toor-nay

*Jean **s'entraîne.***
Jean is training.

to type
taper
ta-pay

to understand
comprendre
kom-prahn-druh

to undress
se déshabiller
suh day-sa-bee-yay

to unpack
déballer
day-bal-lay

to use
utiliser
ew-tee-lee-zay

to visit
visiter
vee-zee-tay

to wait
attendre
at-tahn-druh

to wake up
se réveiller
suh ray-vay-yay

to walk
marcher
mar-shay

Pierre **tape** sur son clavier.
Pierre **types** on his keyboard.

Manon **lave** la vaisselle.
Manon **washes** the dishes.

to want
vouloir
vool-wahr

to warm
réchauffer
ray-shoh-fay

to wash
laver
la-vay

to wash (oneself)
se laver
suh la-vay
I wash
je me lave
zhuh muh lav
you wash
tu te laves
tew tuh lav
he/she washes
il/elle se lave
eel/ehl suh lav
we wash
nous nous lavons
noo noo la-vo(n)
you (plural) wash
vous vous lavez
voo voo la-vay
they wash
ils/elles se lavent
eel/ehl suh lav

to wash the dishes
laver la vaisselle
la-vay la vay-sel

to watch
regarder
ruh-gar-day

to wave
faire un signe de la main
fair a(n) seen-ye duh la ma(n)

to wear
porter
por-tay

to weigh
peser
puh-zay

to whisper
chuchoter
shew-sho-tay

to win
gagner
gan-yay

to wish
souhaiter
sway-tay

to wonder
se demander
suh duh-mahn-day

to work
travailler
tra-va-yay

to work (function)
fonctionner
fonk-syo-nay

to wrap
emballer
ahm-bal-lay

to write
écrire
ay-kreer

Julien **écrit** dans son journal.
Julien **writes** in his journal.

Useful phrases
Expressions utiles

Yes
Oui
wee

No
Non
no(n)

Hello
Bonjour
bon-zhoor

Goodbye
Au revoir
oh ruhv-wahr

See you later
À bientôt
ah byan-toh

Please
S'il te plaît
seel tuh pleh

Thank you
Merci
mair-see

Excuse me
Excuse-moi
eks-kewz mwa

I'm sorry
Je suis désolé
zhuh swee day-zo-lay

My name is...
Je m'appelle...
zhuh ma-pel

I live...
J'habite à...
zha-beet ah

I am... years old.
J'ai... ans.
zhay...ah(n)

I don't understand
Je ne comprends pas
zhuh nuh
kom-prah(n) pah

I don't know
Je ne sais pas
zhuh nuh say pah

Very well
Très bien
treh bya(n)

Bonjour,
je m'appelle Luc.

Learn the days of the week

Monday
lundi
lahn-dee

Tuesday
mardi
mar-dee

Wednesday
mercredi
mair-kruh-dee

Thursday
jeudi
zhuh-dee

Friday
vendredi
vahn-druh-dee

Saturday
samedi
sam-dee

Sunday
dimanche
dee-mahnsh

Very much
Beaucoup
boh-koo

I like/I don't like
J'aime/Je n'aime pas...
zhehm/zhuh nehm pah

Let's go!
Allons-y !
alohn-zee

Happy Birthday!
Bon anniversaire !
bo(n) an-ee-vair-sair

How are you?
Comment ça va ?
ko-mah(n) sa va

What is your name?
Comment t'appelles-tu ?
ko-mah(n) ta-pel tew

Do you speak...?
Parles-tu... ?
parl tew

Do you like...?
Aimes-tu... ?
ehm tew

Do you have...?
As-tu... ?
ah tew

Can I have...?
Puis-je avoir... ?
pwee zhuh av-wahr

How much...?
Combien... ?
kom-bya(n)

What's that?
Qu'est-ce que c'est ?
kess kuh say

How many?
Combien ?
kom-bya(n)

Can you help me?
Peux-tu m'aider ?
puh tew meh-day

What time is it?
Quelle heure est-il ?
kel uhr et eel

Help!
Au secours !
oh suh-koor

Stop!
Arrête !
ar-reht

Turn right/left
Tourne à droite/à gauche
toorn ah drwat/ah gohsh

Go straight on
Va tout droit
va too drwa

In front of
Devant
duh-vah(n)

Next to
À côté de
ah koh-tay duh

Where is/are...?
Où est/sont... ?
oo eh/so(n)

Allons-y !

Learn the months of the year

January
janvier
zhahnv-yay

February
février
fay-vree-yay

March
mars
mars

April
avril
av-reel

May
mai
may

June
juin
zhwa(n)

July
juillet
zhwee-yay

August
août
oot

September
septembre
sep-tahm-bruh

October
octobre
ok-to-bruh

November
novembre
no-vahm-bruh

December
décembre
day-sahm-bruh

Les nombres

Numbers

0	**zéro** *zay-roh* zero	**10**	**dix** *deess* ten	**20**	**vingt** *va(n)* twenty
1	**un** *a(n)* one	**11**	**onze** *onz* eleven	**21**	**vingt et un** *vant ay a(n)* twenty-one
2	**deux** *duh* two	**12**	**douze** *dooz* twelve	**30**	**trente** *trahnt* thirty
3	**trois** *trwa* three	**13**	**treize** *trez* thirteen	**40**	**quarante** *kar-ahnt* forty
4	**quatre** *kat-ruh* four	**14**	**quatorze** *kat-orz* fourteen	**50**	**cinquante** *sank-ahnt* fifty
5	**cinq** *sank* five	**15**	**quinze** *kanz* fifteen	**60**	**soixante** *swa-sahnt* sixty
6	**six** *seess* six	**16**	**seize** *sez* sixteen	**70**	**soixante-dix** *swa-sahnt-deess* seventy
7	**sept** *set* seven	**17**	**dix-sept** *dees-set* seventeen	**80**	**quatre-vingt** *kat-ruh-va(n)* eighty
8	**huit** *weet* eight	**18**	**dix-huit** *deez-weet* eighteen	**90**	**quatre-vingt-dix** *kat-ruh-va(n)-deess* ninety
9	**neuf** *nuhf* nine	**19**	**dix-neuf** *dees-nuhf* nineteen	**100**	**cent** *sah(n)* hundred

Acknowledgements

DK would like to thank the following people:
Sarah Ponder and Carole Oliver for design help;
Marie Greenwood, Jennie Morris, and Sonam Mathur
for editorial help; Angela Wilkes for language
consultancy; Katherine Northam for digital artwork;
Rose Horridge for picture research; Rachael Swann
for picture research assistance; and Hope Annets,
Mary Mead, Bethany Tombs, Todd and Sophie
Yonwin for modelling.
The publisher would like to thank the following for
their kind permission to reproduce their
photographs:
(Key: a-above; b-below/bottom; c-centre; f-far;
l-left; r-right; t-top)
4 Dreamstime.com: Thomas Perkins (tr).
11 Dreamstime.com: Tomasz Markowski (b).
24 Dreamstime.com: Denis Raev (b). 25 Macduff
Everton (tl). 29 Jason Horowitz: Zefa (br). 29
Dreamstime.com: Buriy (tc). 29 Anna Peisl: Zefa
(cr). 29 Getty Images: The Image Bank (bl). 29 DK
Images: Stephen Oliver (tl). 47 Taxi (tr). 51 Science
Photo Library: Phototake Inc. (tr). 62 Dreamstime.
com: Anna501 (bl). 70 Corbis: Photolibrary (cla).
72 Getty Images: Stone/Stuart Westmorland (tl).
82 Indianapolis Motor Speedway Foundation,
Inc. (tc). 88 Fotolia: Picsfive (br). 91 David Edge
(tc). 91 Courtesy of Junior Department, Royal
College of Music, London (br). 115 Dreamstime.
com: Stacy Barnett (tl). 119 Dreamstime.com:
Stockyimages (tc). 122–123RF.com: ka2shka
(bl). 124 Dreamstime.com: Jarenwicklund
(bc). 127 iStockphoto.com: aabejon (bc).
All other images © Dorling Kindersley.
For further information see: www.dkimages.com